Charles Lamb

The Adventures of Ulysses

Charles Lamb

The Adventures of Ulysses

ISBN/EAN: 9783337176563

Printed in Europe, USA, Canada, Australia, Japan

Cover: Foto ©ninafisch / pixelio.de

More available books at **www.hansebooks.com**

THE ADVENTURES OF ULYSSES.

BY

CHARLES LAMB.

EDITED, WITH NOTES, FOR SCHOOLS.

BOSTON:
PUBLISHED BY GINN & COMPANY.
1886.

Entered, according to Act of Congress, in the year 1886, by
GINN & COMPANY,
in the Office of the Librarian of Congress, at Washington.

J. S. CUSHING & CO., PRINTERS, BOSTON.

CONTENTS.

CHAPTER I.

The Cicons. — The Fruit of the Lotos-tree. — Polyphemus and the Cyclops. — The Kingdom of the Winds, and God Æolus's Fatal Present. — The Læstrygonian Man-eaters . . . . . .

CHAPTER II.

The House of Circe. — Men changed into Beasts. — The Voyage to the Underworld. — The Banquet of the Dead . . . . .

CHAPTER III.

The Songs of the Sirens. — Scylla and Charybdis. — The Oxen of the Sun. — The Judgment. — The Crew killed by Lightning . . . .

CHAPTER IV.

The Island of Calypso. — Immortality Refused . . . .

CHAPTER V.

The Tempest. — The Sea-bird's Gift. — The Escape by Swimming. — The Sleep in the Woods . . . .

CHAPTER VI.

The Princess Nausicaa. — The Washing. — The Game with the Ball. — The Court of Phæacia and King Alcinous . . . .

CONTENTS.

CHAPTER VII.

The Songs of Demodocus. — The Convoy Home. — The Mariners Transformed to Stone. — The Young Shepherd 62

CHAPTER VIII.

The Change from a King to a Beggar. — Eumaeus and the Herdsmen. — Telemachus 73

CHAPTER IX.

The Queen's Suitors. — The Battle of the Beggars. — The Armor taken down. — The Meeting with Penelope 89

CHAPTER X.

The Madness from Above. — The Bow of Ulysses. — The Slaughter. — The Conclusion 100

HOMER AND THE ODYSSEY.

AN antique bust represents Homer as a "blind, venerable man, his forehead radiant with high thoughts, his face worn with the fervor of their long strain and stress."

That likeness, and a few traditions, tell us all that we know of the great poet.

When he was born, or where, or how he lived, are mysteries which we cannot hope to solve.

The utmost we can learn is that he was a native of some part of Greece, and that upwards of a thousand years before Christ he was known as the singer of the siege of Troy and of the adventures of Ulysses, in a country where books had not yet begun to be; nay, where there was yet no art of writing and no alphabet even, but where the poet wandered from place to place, reciting his moving verses, as the Egyptian Arabs still recite the stories of the Arabian Nights, to groups of wondering listeners sitting in a circle round their camp-fires on the sands.

The legends which have come down to us describe the Poet as poor as well as blind, and as one whose greatness, like that of Shakespeare, was not fully recognized till after he was gone, so that the familiar lines may, perhaps, be true, which say: —

>"Seven wealthy towns contend for Homer dead,
>Through which the living Homer begged his bread."

It has been conjectured, with apparent good reason, that he must have at one time known what battles were from experience, or he could not have described the contests of the Greeks and Trojans with such vivid power; and that he must also have roamed through many lands, or he could not have given us such a picture of the journeyings and exploits of Ulysses.

Some have even supposed that in the hero of the "Odyssey" we have the best portrait of Homer himself. If so, we know that he was not simply a poet, but, like Ulysses, a man "of many resources and many devices"—a sort of Greek Yankee, always equal to the occasion, who could fight, sing, or flatter his way through all difficulties, and was sure of success in the end.

To understand and enjoy this little book of Charles Lamb's, one must know something of what precedes it.

Within a few years an indefatigable German, digging in the soil of Asia Minor on a part of the coast not far from the straits of Dardanelles, has brought to light not only extensive ruins, but also arms and jewels. He believes these belonged to the King of ancient Troy, or Ilias, that walled city which the Greeks besieged in order to regain the beautiful Helen, wife of one of their countrymen, whom a prince of Troy had carried off with him a too willing captive. The "Iliad" of Homer is the story of the siege of the city and the victory of the Greeks. The sequel to it is the attempt of Ulysses, or Odysseus, one of the Greek heroes, to reach his home in the little island of Ithaca, where he was king. This forms the poem of the "Odyssey," called after his Greek name. The account, as our author gives it, opens after Ulysses has left the island of Calypso in the Mediterranean, where he was shipwrecked, and where, at the entreaty of its queen, he had long remained.

The metre and movement of the poem are the same as that of Longfellow's "Evangeline"; and if in reading the description of Ulysses, when he reveals himself to the terrified suitors in his palace in Ithaca, we read as follows, we shall get an idea of the force and fire of Homer's true style, which may awaken a desire to know more:—

"Thereupon, stripping his tatters away, many-counselled Ulysses
  Strode to the threshold, and stood there, upholding his bow, and his quiver
  Brim-full of shafts; on the ground he poured forth the light-wingèd arrows
  All in a pile at his feet, then turned to the suitors, and spake this:
  'Yonder match has been played; ye have seen my skill at the target:
  Now I will shoot a shot that no man, I fancy, will better,
  Into a different mark—if I may—and Apollo shall aid me.'"

D. H. M.

THE ADVENTURES OF ULYSSES.

CHAPTER I.

The Cicons. — The Fruit of the Lotus-tree. — Polyphemus and the Cyclops. — The Kingdom of the Winds, and God Æolus's Fatal Present. — The Læstrygonian Man-eaters.

THIS history tells of the wanderings of Ulysses and his followers in their return from Troy, after the destruction of that famous city of Asia by the Grecians. He was inflamed with a desire of seeing again, after a ten years' absence, his wife and native country, Ithaca. He was king of a barren spot, and a poor country in comparison with the fruitful plains of Asia, which he was leaving, or with the wealthy kingdoms which he touched upon in his return; yet, wherever he came, he could never see a soil which appeared in his eyes half so sweet or desirable as his country earth. This made him refuse the offers of the goddess Calypso to stay with her, and partake of her immortality in the delightful island; and this gave him strength to break from the enchantments of Circe, the daughter of the Sun.

Cicons (Cĭk′-ons).   Polyphemus (Pŏl-ў-phe′-mus).
Æolus (Ē′-ŏl-us).   Læstrygonian (Lĕs-trў-gō′-ni-an).
Troy: the scene of the Trojan war, a city of the north-western coast of Asia Minor, a few miles from the sea.
Ithaca: a small island in the Ionian Sea, west of Greece.
Calypso: she reigned over an island of the Mediterranean on which Ulysses was shipwrecked.   Circe (Cir′-ce).

From Troy, ill winds cast Ulysses and his fleet upon the coast of the Cicons, a people hostile to the Grecians. Landing his forces, he laid siege to the chief city, Ismarus, which he took, and with it much spoil, and slew many people. But success proved fatal to him; for his soldiers, elated with the spoil, and the good store of provisions which they found in that place, fell to eating and drinking, forgetful of their safety, till the Cicons, who inhabited the coast, had time to assemble their friends and allies from the interior; who, mustering in prodigious force, set upon the Grecians, while they negligently revelled and feasted, and slew many of them, and recovered the spoil. They, dispirited and thinned in their numbers, with difficulty made their retreat good to the ships.

Thence they set sail, sad at heart, yet something cheered that with such fearful odds against them they had not all been utterly destroyed. A dreadful tempest ensued, which for two nights and two days tossed them about, but the third day the weather cleared, and they had hopes of a favorable gale to carry them to Ithaca; but, as they doubled the Cape of Malea, suddenly a north wind arising drove them back as far as Cythera. After that, for the space of nine days, contrary winds continued to drive them in an opposite direction to the point to which they were bound, and the tenth day they put in at a shore where a race of men dwell that are sustained by the fruit of the lotos-tree. Here Ulysses sent some of his men to land for fresh water, who were met by certain of the inhabitants, that gave them some of their country food to eat — not with any ill intention towards them,

Ismarus (Is'-mă-rus).   **Malea (Ma'-le-a).**   **Cythera (Cȳ-thē'-ra).**

though in the event it proved pernicious; for, having eaten of this fruit, so pleasant it proved to their appetite that they in a minute quite forgot all thoughts of home, or of their countrymen, or of ever returning to the ships to give an account of what sort of inhabitants dwelt there, but they would needs stay and live there among them, and eat of that precious food forever; and when Ulysses sent other of his men to look for them, and to bring them back by force, they strove, and wept, and would not leave their food for heaven itself, so much the pleasure of that enchanting food had bewitched them. But Ulysses caused them to be bound hand and foot, and cast under the hatches; and set sail with all possible speed from that baneful coast, lest others after them might taste the lotus, which had such strange qualities to make men forget their native country and the thoughts of home.

Coasting on all that night by unknown and out-of-the-way shores, they came by daybreak to the land where the Cyclops dwell, a sort of giant shepherds that neither sow nor plough, but the earth untilled produces for them rich wheat and barley and grapes, yet they have neither bread nor wine, nor know the arts of cultivation, nor care to know them; for they live each man to himself, without laws or government, or anything like a state or kingdom; but their dwellings are in caves, on the steep heads of mountains; every man's household governed by his own caprice, or not governed at all; their wives and children as lawless as themselves, none caring for others, but each doing as he or she thinks good. Ships or boats they have none, nor artificers to make them, no trade or commerce, or wish to visit other shores; yet they have convenient places for harbors and for shipping. Here Ulysses with a chosen party of twelve followers landed, to explore what sort of men dwelt there, whether hospitable and friendly to strangers, or altogether wild and savage, for as yet no dwellers appeared in sight.

The first sign of habitation which they came to was a giant's cave rudely fashioned, but of a size which betokened the vast proportions of its owner; the pillars which supported it being the bodies of huge oaks or pines, in the natural state of the tree, and all about showed more marks of strength than skill in whoever built it. Ulysses, entering it, admired the savage contrivances and artless structure of the place, and longed to see the tenant of so outlandish a mansion; but well conjecturing that gifts would have more avail in extracting courtesy than strength would succeed in forcing it, from such a one as he expected to find the inhabitant, he resolved to flatter his hospitality with a present of Greek wine, of which he had store in twelve great vessels, so strong that no one ever drank it without an infusion of twenty parts of water to one of wine, yet the fragrance of it even then so delicious that it would have vexed a man who smelled it to abstain from tasting it; but whoever tasted it, it was able to raise his courage to the height of heroic deeds. Taking with them a goat-skin flagon full of this precious liquor, they ventured into the recesses of the cave. Here they pleased themselves a whole day with beholding the giant's kitchen, where the flesh of sheep and goats lay strewed; his dairy, where goat-milk stood ranged in troughs and pails; his pens, where he kept his live animals; but those, he had driven forth to pasture with him when he went out in the morning. While they were feasting their eyes with a

Goat-skin flagon: a vessel for carrying wine made of the skin of a goat.

sight of these curiosities, their ears were suddenly deafened with a noise like the falling of a house. It was the owner of the cave, who had been abroad all day feeding his flock, as his custom was, in the mountains, and now drove them home in the evening from pasture. He threw down a pile of fire-wood, which he had been gathering against supper-time, before the mouth of the cave, which occasioned the crash they heard. The Grecians hid themselves in the remote parts of the cave at sight of the uncouth monster. It was Polyphemus, the largest and savagest of the Cyclops, who boasted himself to be the son of Neptune. He looked more like a mountain crag than a man, and to his brutal body he had a brutish mind answerable. He drove his flock, all that gave milk, to the interior of the cave, but left the rams and the he-goats without. Then taking up a stone so massy that twenty oxen could not have drawn it, he placed it at the mouth of the cave, to defend the entrance, and sat him down to milk his ewes and his goats; which done, he lastly kindled a fire, and throwing his great eye round the cave (for the Cyclops have no more than one eye, and that placed in the midst of their forehead), by the glimmering light he discerned some of Ulysses's men.

"Ho! guests, what are you? Merchants or wandering thieves?" he bellowed out in a voice which took from them all power of reply, it was so astounding.

Only Ulysses summoned resolution to answer, that they came neither for plunder nor traffic, but were Grecians who had lost their way, returning from Troy; which famous city, under the conduct of Agamemnon, the renowned son of Atreus, they had sacked, and laid level with the

Neptune: god of the sea.   Atreus (A'-treus).

ground. Yet now they prostrated themselves humbly before his feet, whom they acknowledged to be mightier than they, and besought him that he would bestow the rites of hospitality upon them, for that Jove was the avenger of wrongs done to strangers, and would fiercely resent any injury which they might suffer.

"Fool!" said the Cyclop, "to come so far to preach to me the fear of the gods. We Cyclops care not for your Jove, whom you fable to be nursed by a goat, nor any of your blessed ones. We are stronger than they, and dare bid open battle to Jove himself, though you and all your fellows of the earth join with him." And he bade them tell him where their ship was in which they came, and whether they had any companions. But Ulysses, with a wise caution, made answer that they had no ship or companions, but were unfortunate men, whom the sea, splitting their ship in pieces, had dashed upon his coast, and they alone had escaped. He replied nothing, but griping two of the nearest of them, as if they had been no more than children, he dashed their brains out against the earth, and, shocking to relate, tore in pieces their limbs, and devoured them yet warm and trembling, making a lion's meal of them, lapping the blood; for the Cyclops are *man-eaters*, and esteem human flesh to be a delicacy far above goat's or kid's; though by reason of their abhorred customs few men approach their coast, except some stragglers, or now and then a shipwrecked mariner. At a sight so horrid, Ulysses and his men were like distracted people. He, when he had made an end of his wicked supper, drained a draught of goat's milk down his prodigious throat, and lay down and slept among his goats. Then

Jove: the greatest of the gods.

Ulysses drew his sword, and half resolved to thrust it with all his might in at the bosom of the sleeping monster; but wiser thoughts restrained him, else they had there without help all perished, for none but Polyphemus himself could have removed that mass of stone which he had placed to guard the entrance. So they were constrained to abide all that night in fear.

When day came, the Cyclop awoke, and kindling a fire, made his breakfast of two other of his unfortunate prisoners, then milked his goats as he was accustomed, and pushing aside the vast stone, and shutting it again when he had done, upon the prisoners, with as much ease as a man opens and shuts a quiver's lid, he let out his flock, and drove them before him with whistlings (as sharp as winds in storms) to the mountains.

Then Ulysses, of whose strength or cunning the Cyclop seems to have had as little heed as of an infant's, being left alone, with the remnant of his men which the Cyclop had not devoured, gave manifest proof how far manly wisdom excels brutish force. He chose a stake from among the wood which the Cyclop had piled up for firing, in length and thickness like a mast, which he sharpened and hardened in the fire, and selected four men, and instructed them what they should do with this stake, and made them perfect in their parts.

When the evening was come, the Cyclop drove home his sheep; and as fortune directed it, either of purpose, or that his memory was overruled by the gods to his hurt (as in the issue it proved), he drove the males of his flock, contrary to his custom, along with the dams into the pens. Then shutting-to the stone of the cave, he fell to his horrible supper. When he had despatched two more of the

Grecians, Ulysses waxed bold with the contemplation of his project, and took a bowl of Greek wine, and merrily dared the Cyclop to drink.

"Cyclop," he said, "take a bowl of wine from the hand of your guest: it may serve to digest the man's flesh that you have eaten, and show what drink our ship held before it went down. All I ask in recompense, if you find it good, is to be dismissed in a whole skin. Truly you must look to have few visitors, if you observe this new custom of eating your guests."

The brute took and drank, and vehemently enjoyed the taste of wine, which was new to him, and swilled again at the flagon, and entreated for more, and prayed Ulysses to tell him his name, that he might bestow a gift upon the man who had given him such brave liquor. The Cyclops, he said, had grapes, but this rich juice, he swore, was simply divine. Again Ulysses plied him with the wine, and the fool drank it as fast as he poured out, and again he asked the name of his benefactor, which Ulysses, cunningly dissembling, said, "My name is Noman: my kindred and friends in my own country call me Noman." "Then," said the Cyclop, "this is the kindness I will show thee, Noman: I will eat thee last of all thy friends." He had scarce expressed his savage kindness, when the fumes of the strong wine overcame him, and he reeled down upon the floor and sank into a dead sleep.

Ulysses watched his time, while the monster lay insensible, and, heartening up his men, they placed the sharp end of the stake in the fire till it was heated red-hot, and some god gave them a courage beyond that which they were used to have, and the four men with difficulty bored the sharp end of the huge stake, which they had heated red-hot, right into the eye of the drunken cannibal, and Ulysses helped to thrust it in with all his might, still farther and farther, with effort, as men bore with an auger, till the scalded blood gushed out, and the eye-ball smoked, and the strings of the eye cracked, as the burning rafter broke in it, and the eye hissed, as hot iron hisses when it is plunged into water.

He, waking, roared with the pain so loud that all the cavern broke into claps like thunder. They fled, and dispersed into corners. He plucked the burning stake from his eye, and hurled the wood madly about the cave. Then he cried out with a mighty voice for his brethren the Cyclops, that dwelt hard by in caverns upon hills; they, hearing the terrible shout, came flocking from all parts to inquire, What ailed Polyphemus? and what cause he had for making such horrid clamors in the night-time to break their sleeps? if his fright proceeded from any mortal? if strength or craft had given him his death's blow? He made answer from within that Noman had hurt him, Noman had killed him, Noman was with him in the cave. They replied, "If no man has hurt thee, and no man is with thee, then thou art alone, and the evil that afflicts thee is from the hand of Heaven, which none can resist or help." So they left him and went their way, thinking that some disease troubled him. He, blind and ready to split with the anguish of the pain, went groaning up and down in the dark, to find the door-way, which when he found, he removed the stone, and sat in the threshold, feeling if he could lay hold on any man going out with the sheep, which (the day now breaking) were beginning to issue forth to their accustomed pastures. But Ulysses, whose first artifice in giving himself that ambiguous name had succeeded so well with the Cyclop, was not of a wit so gross to be caught by that palpable device. But casting about in his mind all the ways which he could contrive for escape (no less than all their lives depending on the success), at last he thought of this expedient. He made knots of the osier twigs upon which the Cyclop commonly slept; with which he tied the fattest and fleeciest of the rams together, three in a rank, and under the middle ram he tied a man, and himself last, wrapping himself fast with both hands in the rich wool of one, the fairest of the flock.

And now the sheep began to issue forth very fast; the males went first, the females, unmilked, stood by, bleating and requiring the hand of their shepherd in vain to milk them. Still, as the males passed, he felt the backs of those fleecy fools, never dreaming that they carried his enemies under them; so they passed on till the last ram came loaded with his wool and Ulysses together. He stopped that ram and felt him, and had his hand once in the hair of Ulysses, yet knew it not, and he chid the ram for being last, and spoke to it as if it understood him, and asked it whether it did not wish that its master had his eye again, which that abominable Noman with his execrable rout had put out, when they had got him down with wine; and he willed the ram to tell him whereabouts in the cave his enemy lurked, that he might dash his brains and strew them about, to ease his heart of that tormenting revenge which rankled in it. After a deal of such foolish talk to the beast, he let it go.

When Ulysses found himself free, he let go his hold, and assisted in disengaging his friends. The rams which had befriended them they carried off with them to the ships, where their companions with tears in their eyes received them, as men escaped from death. They plied their oars, and set their sails, and when they were got as far off from shore as a voice could reach, Ulysses cried out to the Cyclop: "Cyclop, thou shouldst not have so much abused thy monstrous strength, as to devour thy guests. Jove by my hand sends thee requital to pay thy savage inhumanity." The Cyclop heard, and came forth enraged, and in his anger he plucked a fragment of a rock, and threw it with blind fury at the ships. It narrowly escaped lighting upon the bark in which Ulysses sat, but with the fall it raised so fierce an ebb as bore back the ship till it almost touched the shore. "Cyclop," said Ulysses, "if any ask thee who imposed on thee that unsightly blemish in thine eye, say it was Ulysses, son of Laertes: the king of Ithaca am I called, the waster of cities." Then they crowded sail, and beat the old sea, and forth they went with a forward gale; sad for former losses, yet glad to have escaped at any rate; till they came to the isle where Æolus reigned, who is god of the winds.

Here Ulysses and his men were courteously received by the monarch, who showed him his twelve children which have rule over the twelve winds. A month they stayed and feasted with him, and at the end of the month he dismissed them with many presents, and gave to Ulysses at parting an ox's hide, in which were enclosed *all the winds:* only he left abroad the western wind, to play upon their sails and waft them gently home to Ithaca. This bag, bound in a glittering silver band so close that no breath could escape, Ulysses hung up at the mast. His companions did not know its contents, but guessed that the monarch had given to him some treasures of gold or silver.

Nine days they sailed smoothly, favored by the western wind, and by the tenth they approached so nigh as to discern lights kindled on the shores of their country earth: when, by ill-fortune, Ulysses, overcome with fatigue of watching the helm, fell asleep. The mariners seized the opportunity, and one of them said to the rest, "A fine time has this leader of ours; wherever he goes he is sure of presents, when we come away empty-handed; and see what King Æolus has given him, store no doubt of gold and silver." A word was enough to those covetous wretches, who quick as thought untied the bag, and, instead of gold, out rushed with mighty noise *all the winds*. Ulysses with the noise awoke, and saw their mistake, but too late, for the ship was driving with all the winds back far from Ithaca, far as to the island of Æolus from which they had parted, in one hour measuring back what in nine days they had scarcely tracked, and in sight of home too! Up he flew amazed, and, raving, doubted whether he should not fling himself into the sea for grief of his bitter disappointment. At last he hid himself under the hatches for shame. And scarce could he be prevailed upon, when he was told he was arrived again in the harbor of king Æolus, to go himself or send to that monarch for a second succor; so much the disgrace of having misused his royal bounty (though it was the crime of his followers, and not his own) weighed upon him; and when at last he went, and took a herald with him, and came where the god sat on his throne, feasting with his children, he would not thrust in among them at their meat, but set himself down like one unworthy in the threshold.

Indignation seized Æolus to behold him in that manner

Herald : *i.e.*, a person to announce him.

returned; and he said: "Ulysses, what has brought you back? Are you so soon tired of your country; or did not our present please you? We thought we had given you a kingly passport." Ulysses made answer: "My men have done this ill mischief to me; they did it while I slept." "Wretch!" said Æolus, "avaunt, and quit our shores: it fits not us to convoy men whom the gods hate, and will have perish."

Forth they sailed, but with far different hopes than when they left the same harbor the first time with all the winds confined, only the west wind suffered to play upon their sails to waft them in gentle murmurs to Ithaca. They were now the sport of every gale that blew, and despaired of ever seeing home more. Now those covetous mariners were cured of their surfeit for gold, and would not have touched it if it had lain in untold heaps before them.

Six days and nights they drove along, and on the seventh day they put into Lamos, a port of the Læstrygonians. So spacious this harbor was that it held with ease all their fleet, which rode at anchor, safe from any storms, all but the ship in which Ulysses was embarked. He, as if prophetic of the mischance which followed, kept still without the harbor, making fast his bark to a rock at the land's point, which he climbed with purpose to survey the country. He saw a city with smoke ascending from the roofs, but neither ploughs going, nor oxen yoked, nor any sign of agricultural works. Making choice of two men, he sent them to the city to explore what sort of inhabitants dwelt there. His messengers had not gone far before they met a damsel, of stature surpassing human, who was coming to draw water from a spring. They asked her who dwelt in that land. She made no reply, but led them in silence to her father's palace. He was a monarch, and named Antiphas. He and all his people were giants. When they entered the palace, a woman, the mother of the damsel, but far taller than she, rushed abroad and called for Antiphas. He came, and snatching up one of the two men, made as if he would devour him. The other fled. Antiphas raised a mighty shout, and instantly, this way and that, multitudes of gigantic people issued out at the gates, and, making for the harbor, tore up huge pieces of the rocks and flung them at the ships which lay there, all which they utterly overwhelmed and sank; and the unfortunate bodies of men which floated, and which the sea did not devour, these cannibals thrust through with harpoons, like fishes, and bore them off to their dire feast. Ulysses with his single bark, that had never entered the harbor, escaped; that bark which was now the only vessel left of all the gallant navy that had set sail with him from Troy. He pushed off from the shore, cheering the sad remnant of his men, whom horror at the sight of their countrymen's fate had almost turned to marble.

Antiphas (An'-ti-phas).

CHAPTER II.

The House of Circe. — Men changed into Beasts. — The Voyage to the Underworld, or Abode of the Dead. — The Banquet of the Dead.

ON went the single ship till it came to the island of Æa, where Circe, the dreadful daughter of the Sun, dwelt. She was deeply skilled in magic, a haughty beauty, and had hair like the Sun. The Sun was her father, and Perse, daughter to Oceanus, her mother.

Here a dispute arose among Ulysses's men, which of them should go ashore and explore the country; for there was a necessity that some should go to procure water and provisions, their stock of both being nigh spent; but their hearts failed them when they called to mind the shocking fate of their fellows whom the Læstrygonians had eaten, and those which the foul Cyclop Polyphemus had crushed between his jaws; which moved them so tenderly in the recollection that they wept. But tears never yet supplied any man's wants; this Ulysses knew full well, and dividing his men (all that were left) into two companies, at the head of one of which was himself, and at the head of the other Eurylochus, a man of tried courage, he cast lots which of them should go up into the country, and the lot fell upon Eurylochus, and his company, two-and-twenty in number, who took their leave, with tears, of Ulysses and his men that stayed, whose eyes wore the same wet badges of weak humanity,

Æa (E-ē'-a).
Oceanus (O-cē'-ăn-us).
Perse (Per'-se).
Eurylochus (Eu-ryl'-o-kus).

for they surely thought never to see these their companions again, but that on every coast where they should come, they should find nothing but savages and cannibals.

Eurylochus and his party proceeded up the country, till in a dale they descried the house of Circe, built of bright stone, by the roadside. Before her gate lay many beasts, as wolves, lions, leopards, which, by her art, from wild, she had rendered tame. These arose when they saw strangers, and stood upon their hinder paws, and fawned upon Eurylochus and his men, who dreaded the effects of such monstrous kindness; and staying at the gate they heard the enchantress within, sitting at her loom, singing such strains as suspended all mortal faculties, while she wove a web, subtle and glorious, and of texture inimitable on earth, as all the housewiferies of the deities are. Strains so ravishingly sweet provoked even the sagest and prudentest heads among the party to knock and call at the gate. The shining gate the enchantress opened, and bade them come in and feast. They unwise followed, all but Eurylochus, who stayed without the gate, suspicious that some train was laid for them. Being entered, she placed them in chairs of state, and set before them meal and honey, and Smyrna wine, but mixed with baneful drugs of powerful enchantment. When they had eaten of these, and drunk of her cup, she touched them with her charming-rod, and straight they were transformed into swine, having the bodies of swine, the bristles, and snout, and grunting noise of that animal; only they still retained the minds of men, which made them the more to lament their brutish transformation. Having changed them, she shut them up in her sty with many more whom her wicked sorceries had formerly changed, and gave them swine's food — mast, and acorns, and chestnuts — to eat.

Eurylochus, who beheld nothing of these sad changes from where he was stationed without the gate, only instead of his companions that entered (who he thought had all vanished by witchcraft) beheld a herd of swine, hurried back to the ship, to give an account of what he had seen; but so frighted and perplexed, that he could give no distinct report of anything, only he remembered a a palace, and a woman singing at her work, and gates guarded by lions. But his companions, he said, were all vanished.

Then Ulysses, suspecting some foul witchcraft, snatched his sword and his bow, and commanded Eurylochus instantly to lead him to the place. But Eurylochus fell down, and, embracing his knees, besought him by the name of a man whom the gods had in their protection, not to expose his safety, and the safety of them all, to certain destruction.

"Do thou then stay, Eurylochus," answered Ulysses: "eat thou and drink in the ship in safety; while I go alone upon this adventure: necessity, from whose law is no appeal, compels me."

So saying, he quitted the ship and went on shore, accompanied by none; none had the hardihood to offer to partake that perilous adventure with him, so much they dreaded the enchantments of the witch. Singly he pursued his journey till he came to the shining gates which stood before her mansion; but when he essayed to put his foot over her threshold, he was suddenly stopped by the apparition of a young man, bearing a golden rod in his

Mast: beech-nuts, etc.

hand, who was the god Mercury. He held Ulysses by the wrist, to stay his entrance; and "Whither wouldest thou go?" he said, "O thou most erring of the sons of men! knowest thou not that this is the house of great Circe, where she keeps thy friends in a loathsome sty, changed from the fair forms of men into the detestable and ugly shapes of swine? art thou prepared to share their fate, from which nothing can ransom thee?" But neither his words nor his coming from heaven could stop the daring foot of Ulysses, whom compassion for the misfortune of his friends had rendered careless of danger: which when the god perceived, he had pity to see valor so misplaced, and gave him the flower of the herb *moly*, which is sovereign against enchantments. The moly is a small unsightly root, its virtues but little known and in low estimation; the dull shepherd treads on it every day with his clouted shoes; but it bears a small white flower, which is medicinal against charms, blights, mildews, and damps. "Take this in thy hand," said Mercury, "and with it boldly enter her gates; when she shall strike thee with her rod, thinking to change thee, as she has changed thy friends, boldly rush in upon her with thy sword, and extort from her the dreadful oath of the gods, that she will use no enchantments against thee; then force her to restore thy abused companions." He gave Ulysses the little white flower, and, instructing him how to use it, vanished.

When the god was departed, Ulysses with loud knockings beat at the gate of the palace. The shining gates were opened, as before, and great Circe with hospitable cheer invited in her guest. She placed him on a throne with

Clouted: studded with hob-nails.

more distinction than she had used to his fellows; she mingled wine in a costly bowl, and he drank of it, mixed with those poisonous drugs. When he had drunk, she struck him with her charming-rod, and "To your sty!" she cried; "out, swine! mingle with your companions!" But those powerful words were not proof against the preservative which Mercury had given to Ulysses; he remained unchanged, and, as the god had directed him, boldly charged the witch with his sword, as if he meant to take her life; which when she saw, and perceived that her charms were weak against the antidote which Ulysses bore about him, she cried out and bent her knees beneath his sword, embracing his, and said, "Who or what manner of man art thou? Never drank any man before thee of this cup but he repented it in some brute's form. Thy shape remains unaltered as thy mind. Thou canst be none other than Ulysses, renowned above all the world for wisdom, whom the Fates have long since decreed that I must love. This haughty bosom bends to thee. O Ithacan, a goddess wooes thee."

"O Circe," he replied, "how canst thou treat of love or marriage with one whose friends thou hast turned into beasts? and now offerest him thy hand in wedlock, only that thou mightest have him in thy power, to live the life of a beast with thee, effeminate, subject to thy will, perhaps to be advanced in time to the honor of a place in thy sty. What pleasure canst thou promise which may tempt the soul of a reasonable man? Thy meats, spiced with poison; or thy wines, drugged with death? Thou must swear to me that thou wilt never attempt against me the treasons which thou hast practised upon my friends." The enchantress, won by the terror of his threats, or by the violence of that new love which she felt kindling in her veins for him, swore by Styx, the great oath of the gods, that she meditated no injury to him. Then Ulysses made show of gentler treatment, which gave her hopes of inspiring him with a passion equal to that which she felt. She called her handmaids, four that served her in chief, who were daughters to her silver fountains, to her sacred rivers, and to her consecrated woods, to deck her apartments, to spread rich carpets, and set her silver tables with dishes of the purest gold, and meat as precious as that which the gods eat, to entertain her guest. One brought water to wash his feet, and one brought wine to chase away, with a refreshing sweetness, the sorrows that had come of late so thick upon him, and hurt his noble mind. They strewed perfumes on his head, and, after he had bathed in a bath of the choicest aromatics, they brought him rich and costly apparel to put on. Then he was conducted to a throne of massy silver, and a regale, fit for Jove when he banquets, was placed before him. But the feast which Ulysses desired was to see his friends (the partners of his voyage) once more in the shapes of men; and the food which could give him nourishment must be taken in at his eyes. Because he missed this sight, he sat melancholy and thoughtful, and would taste of none of the rich delicacies placed before him. Which when Circe noted, she easily divined the cause of his sadness, and leaving the seat in which she sat throned, went to her sty, and let abroad his men, who came in like swine, and filled the ample hall, where Ulysses sat, with gruntings. Hardly had he time to let his sad eye run over their altered forms and brutal metamorphosis, when, with an ointment which she smeared over them,

Styx: a river of the underworld, or abode of the dead.
Metamorphosis (met-a-mor′-pho-sis).

suddenly their bristles fell off, and they started up in their own shapes, men as before. They knew their leader again, and clung about him, with joy of their late restoration, and some shame for their late change; and wept so loud, blubbering out their joy in broken accents, that the palace was filled with a sound of pleasing mourning, and the witch herself, great Circe, was not unmoved at the sight. To make her atonement complete, she sent for the remnant of Ulysses's men who stayed behind at the ship, giving up their great commander for lost; who when they came, and saw him again alive, circled with their fellows, no expression can tell what joy they felt; they even cried out with rapture, and to have seen their frantic expressions of mirth a man might have supposed that they were just in sight of their native country, the cliffs of rocky Ithaca. Only Eurylochus would hardly be persuaded to enter that palace of wonders, for he remembered with a kind of horror how his companions had vanished from his sight.

Then great Circe spake, and gave order that there should be no more sadness among them, nor remembering of past sufferings. For as yet they fared like men that are exiles from their country, and if a gleam of mirth shot among them, it was suddenly quenched with the thought of their helpless and homeless condition. Her kind persuasions wrought upon Ulysses and the rest, that they spent twelve months in all manner of delight with her in her palace. For Circe was a powerful magician, and could command the moon from her sphere, or unroot the solid oak from its place to make it dance for their diversion, and by the help of her illusions she could vary the taste of pleasures, and contrive delights, recreations, and jolly pastimes, to "fetch the day about from sun to sun, and rock the tedious year as in a delightful dream."

At length Ulysses awoke from the trance of the faculties into which her charms had thrown him, and the thought of home returned with tenfold vigor to goad and sting him; that home where he had left his virtuous wife Penelope, and his young son Telemachus. One day when Circe had been lavish of her caresses, and was in her kindest humor, he moved to her subtly, and as it were afar off, the question of his home-return; to which she answered firmly, "O Ulysses, it is not in my power to detain one whom the gods have destined to further trials. But leaving me, before you pursue your journey home, you must visit the house of Ades, or Death, to consult the shade of Tiresias the Theban prophet; to whom alone, of all the dead, Proserpine, queen of the underworld, has committed the secret of future events: it is he that must inform you whether you shall ever see again your wife and country." "O Circe," he cried, "that is impossible: who shall steer my course to Pluto's kingdom? Never ship had strength to make that voyage." "Seek no guide," she replied; "but raise you your mast, and hoist your white sails, and sit in your ship in peace: the north wind shall waft you through the seas, till you shall cross the expanse of the ocean and come to where grow the poplar groves and willows pale of Proserpine: where Pyriphlegethon and Cocytus and Acheron mingle their waves. Cocytus is an arm of Styx, the

---

Penelope (Pĕ-nĕl'-o-pe).   Telemachus (Tĕ-lem'-ă-kus).
Ades (Ā'-dēs).   Tiresias (Ti-re'-si-as).
Proserpine (Prŏ-ser'-pĭ-nĕ).

Raise you your mast: the so-called ships of Ulysses were simply large sail-boats; the masts were taken out and laid down in the boats on landing, and the boats themselves were often drawn on shore.

Pyriphlegethon (Pў-ri-phleg'-ĕ-thŏn), **Cocytus** (Cō-cȳ'-tus), **Acheron** (Ăk'-ĕ-ron): tributaries of rivers of the underworld.

forgetful river. Here dig a pit, and make it a cubit broad and a cubit long, and pour in milk, and honey, and wine, and the blood of a ram, and the blood of a black ewe, and turn away thy face while thou pourest in, and the dead shall come flocking to taste the milk and the blood; but suffer none to approach thy offering till thou hast inquired of Tiresias all which thou wishest to know."

He did as great Circe had appointed. He raised his mast, and hoisted his white sails, and sat in his ship in peace. The north wind wafted him through the seas, till he crossed the ocean, and came to the sacred woods of Proserpine. He stood at the confluence of the three floods, and digged a pit, as she had given directions, and poured in his offering — the blood of a ram, and the blood of a black ewe, milk, and honey, and wine; and the dead came to his banquet; aged men, and women, and youths, and children who died in infancy. But none of them would he suffer to approach, and dip their thin lips in the offering, till Tiresias was served, not though his own mother was among the number, whom now for the first time he knew to be dead, for he had left her living when he went to Troy, and she had died since his departure, and the tidings never reached him; though it irked his soul to use constraint upon her, yet in compliance with the injunction of great Circe he forced her to retire along with the other ghosts. Then Tiresias, who bore a golden sceptre, came and lapped of the offering, and immediately he knew Ulysses, and began to prophesy: *he denounced woe to Ulysses — woe, woe, and many sufferings — through the anger of Neptune for the putting out of the eye of the sea-god's son. Yet there was safety after suffering, if they could ab-*

Cubit: the length of the fore-arm, about a foot and a half.

stain from slaughtering the oxen of the Sun after they landed in the Triangular island.* For Ulysses, the gods had destined him from a king to become a beggar, and to perish by his own guests, unless he slew those who knew him not.

This prophecy, ambiguously delivered, was all that Tiresias was empowered to unfold, or else there was no longer place for him; for now the souls of the other dead came flocking in such numbers, tumultuously demanding the blood, that freezing horror seized the limbs of the living Ulysses, to see so many, and all dead, and he the only one alive in that region. Now his mother came and lapped the blood, without restraint from her son, and now she knew him to be her son, and inquired of him why he had come alive to their comfortless habitations. And she said that affliction for Ulysses's long absence had preyed upon her spirits, and brought her to the grave.

Ulysses's soul melted at her moving narration, and forgetting the state of the dead, and that the airy texture of disembodied spirits does not admit of the embraces of flesh and blood, he threw his arms about her to clasp her: the poor ghost melted from his embrace, and, looking mournfully upon him, vanished away.

But now came a mournful ghost, that late was Agamemnon, son of Atreus, the mighty leader of all the host of Greece and their confederate kings that warred against Troy. He came with the rest to sip a little of the blood at that uncomfortable banquet. Ulysses was moved with compassion to see him among them, and asked him what untimely fate had brought him there, if storms had overwhelmed him coming from Troy, or if he had perished in some mutiny by his own soldiers at a division of the prey.

The Triangular Island: Sicily.

"By none of these," he replied, "did I come to my death; but slain at a banquet to which I was invited by Ægisthus after my return home. He conspiring with my wife, they laid a scheme for my destruction, training me forth to a banquet as an ox goes to the slaughter, and, there surrounding me, they slew me with all my friends about me.

"Clytemnestra, my wicked wife, forgetting the vows which she swore to me in wedlock, would not lend a hand to close my eyes in death. But nothing is so heaped with impieties as such a woman, who would kill her spouse that married her a maid. When I brought her home to my house a bride, I hoped in my heart that she would be loving to me and my children. Now, her black treacheries have cast a foul aspersion on her whole sex. Blessed husbands will have their loving wives in suspicion for her bad deeds."

"Alas!" said Ulysses, "there seems to be a fatality in your royal house of Atreus, and that they are hated of Jove for their wives. For Helen's sake, your brother Menelaus's wife, what multitudes fell in the wars of Troy!"

Agamemnon replied, "For this cause be not thou more kind than wise to any woman. Let not thy words express to her at any time all that is in thy mind, keep still some secrets to thyself. But thou by any bloody contrivances of thy wife never needst fear to fall. Exceeding wise she is, and to her wisdom she has a goodness as eminent; Icarius's daughter, Penelope the chaste: we left her a young bride when we parted from our wives to go to

---

Ægisthus (E-gis'-thus).   **Clytemnestra** (Clyt-em-nes'-tra).
Menelaus (Měn-ě-lā'-us).   **Icarius** (I-ca'-ri-us).

the wars, with her first child at her breast, the young Telemachus, whom you shall see grown up to manhood on your return, and he shall greet his father with befitting welcomes. My Orestes, my dear son, I shall never see again. His mother has deprived his father of the sight of him, and perhaps will slay him as she slew his sire. It is now no world to trust a woman in. But what says fame? is my son yet alive? lives he in Orchomen, or in Pylus, or is he resident in Sparta, in his uncle's court? As yet, I see, divine Orestes is not here with me."

To this Ulysses replied that he had received no certain tidings where Orestes abode, only some uncertain rumors which he could not report for truth.

While they held this sad conference, with kind tears striving to render unkind fortunes more palatable, the soul of great Achilles joined them. "What desperate adventure has brought Ulysses to these regions," said Achilles; "to see the end of dead men, and their foolish shades?"

Ulysses answered him that he had come to consult Tiresias respecting his voyage home. "But thou, O son of Thetis," said he, "why dost thou disparage the state of the dead? seeing that as alive thou didst surpass all men in glory, thou must needs retain thy pre-eminence here below: so great Achilles triumphs over death."

But Achilles made reply that he had much rather be a peasant-slave upon the earth than reign over all the dead. So much did the inactivity and slothful condition of that state displease his unquenchable and restless spirit. Only he inquired of Ulysses if his father Peleus were living, and how his son Neoptolemus conducted himself.

Orestes (O-res'-tes).   **Orchomen** (Or'-kom-en).   **Pylus** (Pȳl'-us).
Achilles (A-kil'-lēs).   **Thetis** (Thĕt-is).   **Peleus** (Pē-leus).

Of Peleus Ulysses could tell him nothing; but of Neoptolemus he thus bore witness: "From Scyros I convoyed your son by sea to the Greeks: where I can speak of him, for I knew him. He was chief in council, and in the field. When any question was proposed, so quick was his conceit in the forward apprehension of any case, that he ever spoke first, and was heard with more attention than the older heads. Only myself and aged Nestor could compare with him in giving advice. In battle I cannot speak his praise, unless I could count all that fell by his sword. I will only mention one instance of his manhood. When we sat hid within the wooden horse, in the ambush which deceived the Trojans to their destruction, I, who had the management of that stratagem, still shifted my place from side to side to note the behavior of our men. In some I marked their hearts trembling, through all the pains which they took to appear valiant, and in others tears, that in spite of manly courage would gush forth. And to say truth, it was an adventure of high enterprise, and as perilous a stake as was ever played in war's game. But in him I could not observe the least sign of weakness, no tears nor tremblings, but his hand still on his good sword, and ever urging me to set open the machine and let us out before the time was come for doing it; and when we sallied out he was still first in that fierce destruction and bloody midnight desolation of king Priam's city."

This made the soul of Achilles to tread a swifter pace, with high-raised feet, as he vanished away, for the joy which he took in his son being applauded by Ulysses.

A sad shade stalked by, which Ulysses knew to be the

Neoptolemus (Nĕ-op-tŏl′-ĕm-us).   **Conceit:** *i.e.*, understanding.

ghost of Ajax, his opponent, when living, in that famous dispute about the right of succeeding to the arms of the deceased Achilles. They being adjudged by the Greeks to Ulysses, as the prize of wisdom above bodily strength, the noble Ajax in despite went mad, and slew himself. The sight of his rival turned to a shade by his dispute so subdued the passion of emulation in Ulysses that for his sake he wished that judgment in that controversy had been given against himself, rather than so illustrious a chief should have perished for the desire of those arms which his prowess (second only to Achilles in fight) so eminently had deserved. "Ajax," he cried, "all the Greeks mourn for thee as much as they lamented for Achilles. Let not thy wrath burn forever, great son of Telamon. Ulysses seeks peace with thee, and will make any atonement to thee that can appease thy hurt spirit." But the shade stalked on, and would not exchange a word with Ulysses, though he prayed it with many tears and many earnest entreaties. "He might have spoke to me," said Ulysses, "since I spoke to him; but I see the resentments of the dead are eternal."

Then Ulysses saw a throne on which was placed a judge distributing sentence. He that sat on the throne was Minos, and he was dealing out just judgments to the dead. He it is that assigns them their place in bliss or woe.

Then came by a thundering ghost, the large-limbed Orion, the mighty hunter, who was hunting there the ghosts of the beasts which he had slaughtered in desert hills upon the earth. For the dead delight in the occupations which pleased them in the time of their living upon the earth.

Telamon (Těl'-å-mōn). **Minos** (Mī'-nos). **Orion** (Ŏ-rī'-on).

There was Tityus suffering eternal pains. Two vultures sat perpetually preying upon his liver with their crooked beaks; which as fast as they devoured, is forever renewed; nor can he fray them away with his great hands.

There was Tantalus, plagued for his great sins, standing up to his chin in water, which he can never taste, but still as he bows his head, thinking to quench his burning thirst, instead of water he licks up unsavory dust. All fruits pleasant to the sight, and of delicious flavor, hang in ripe clusters about his head, seeming as though they offered themselves to be plucked by him; but when he reaches out his hand, some wind carries them far out of his sight into the clouds: so he is starved in the midst of plenty by the righteous doom of Jove, in memory of that inhuman banquet at which the sun turned pale, when the unnatural father served up the limbs of his little son in a dish, as meat for his divine guests.

There was Sisyphus, that sees no end to his labors. His punishment is, to be forever rolling up a vast stone to the top of a mountain, which, when it gets to the top, falls down with a crushing weight, and all his work is to be begun again. He was bathed all over in sweat, that reeked out a smoke which covered his head like a mist. His crime had been the revealing of state secrets.

There Ulysses saw Hercules — not that Hercules who enjoys immortal life in heaven among the gods, and is married to Hebe or Youth; but his shadow, which remains below. About him the dead flocked as thick as bats, hovering around, and cuffing at his head: he stands with his dreadful bow, ever in the act to shoot.

Tityus (Tĭt′-ĭ-us).   **Sisyphus** (Sĭs′-ĭ-phus).   **Hebe** (Hē′bē).

There also might Ulysses have seen and spoken with the shades of Theseus, and Pirithous, and the old heroes; but he had conversed enough with horrors; therefore, covering his face with his hands, that he might see no more spectres, he resumed his seat in his ship, and pushed off. The bark moved of itself without the help of any oar, and soon brought him out of the regions of death into the cheerful quarters of the living, and to the island of Æaea, whence he had set forth.

Theseus (Thē'-scus). **Pirithous** (Pī-rĭth'-ŏ-us).

CHAPTER III.

The Song of the Sirens. — Scylla and Charybdis. — The Oxen of the Sun. — The Judgment. — The Crew killed by Lightning.

"UNHAPPY man, who at thy birth wast appointed twice to die! others shall die once; but thou, besides that death that remains for thee, common to all men, hast in thy lifetime visited the shades of death. Thee Scylla, thee Charybdis, expect. Thee the deathful Sirens lie in wait for, that taint the minds of whoever listen to them with their sweet singing. Whosoever shall but hear the call of any Siren, he will so despise both wife and children through their sorceries that the stream of his affection never again shall set homewards, nor shall he take joy in wife or children thereafter, or they in him."

With these prophetic greetings great Circe met Ulysses on his return. He besought her to instruct him in the nature of the Sirens, and by what method their baneful allurements were to be resisted.

"They are sisters three," she replied, "that sit in a mead (by which your ship must needs pass) circled with dead men's bones. These are the bones of men whom they have slain, after with fawning invitements they have enticed them into their fen. Yet such is the celestial harmony of their voice accompanying the persuasive magic of their words, that, knowing this, you shall not be

Scylla (Scўl'-la).   Charybdis (Kă-rĭb'-dis).
Mead: a meadow.   Fen: low-land, partly covered with water.

able to withstand their enticements. Therefore, when you are to sail by them, you shall stop the ears of your companions with wax, that they may hear no note of that dangerous music; but for yourself, that you may hear, and yet live, give them strict command to bind you hand and foot to the mast, and in no case to set you free, till you are out of the danger of the temptation, though you should entreat it, and implore it ever so much, but to bind you rather the more for your requesting to be loosed. So shall you escape that snare."

Ulysses then prayed her that she would inform him what Scylla and Charybdis were, which she had taught him by name to fear. She replied: "Sailing from Æaea to Trinacria, you must pass at an equal distance between two fatal rocks. Incline never so little either to the one side or the other, and your ship must meet with certain destruction. No vessel ever yet tried that pass without being lost but the Argo, which owed her safety to the sacred freight she bore, the fleece of the golden-backed ram, which could not perish. The biggest of these rocks which you shall come to, Scylla hath in charge. There in a deep whirlpool at the foot of the rock the abhorred monster shrouds her face; who if she were to show her full form, no eye of man or god could endure the sight: thence she stretches out all her six long necks, peering and diving to suck up fish, dolphins, dog-fish, and whales, whole ships, and their men, whatever comes within her raging gulf. The other rock is lesser, and of less ominous aspect; but there dreadful Charybdis sits, supping the black deeps. Thrice a day she drinks her pits dry, and thrice a day again she belches them all up; but when she

Trinacria (Trī-na'-cri-a).

is drinking, come not nigh, for, being once caught, the force of Neptune cannot redeem you from her swallow. Better trust to Scylla, for she will but have for her six necks six men: Charybdis in her insatiate draught will ask all."

Then Ulysses inquired, in case he should escape Charybdis, whether he might not assail that other monster with his sword; to which she replied that he must not think that he had an enemy subject to death, or wounds, to contend with, for Scylla could never die. Therefore, his best safety was in flight, and to invoke none of the gods but Cratis, who is Scylla's mother, and might perhaps forbid her daughter to devour them. For his conduct after he arrived at Trinacria she referred him to the admonitions which had been given him by Tiresias.

Ulysses having communicated her instructions, as far as related to the Sirens, to his companions, who had not been present at that interview, but concealing from them the rest, as he had done the terrible predictions of Tiresias, that they might not be deterred by fear from pursuing their voyage — the time for departure being come, they set their sails, and took a final leave of great Circe; who by her art calmed the heavens, and gave them smooth seas, and a right fore-wind (the seaman's friend) to bear them on their way to Ithaca.

They had not sailed past a hundred leagues before the breeze which Circe had lent them suddenly stopped. It was stricken dead. All the sea lay in prostrate slumber. Not a gasp of air could be felt. The ship stood still. Ulysses guessed that the island of the Sirens was not far off, and that they had charmed the air so with their dev-

Fore-wind: *i.e.*, a wind which would blow them forward.

ilish singing. Therefore he made him cakes of wax, as Circe had instructed him, and stopped the ears of his men with them; then causing himself to be bound hand and foot, he commanded the rowers to ply their oars and row as fast as speed could carry them past that fatal shore. They soon came within sight of the Sirens, who sang in Ulysses's hearing: —

> Come here, thou, worthy of a world of praise,
> That doth so high the Grecian glory raise;
> Ulysses! stay thy ship; and that song hear
> That none pass'd ever, but it bent his ear,
> But left him ravish'd, and instructed more
> By us than any ever heard before.
> For we know all things, whatsoever were
> In wide Troy labor'd; whatsoever there
> The Grecians and the Trojans both sustain'd,
> By those high issues that the gods ordain'd;
> And whatsoever all the earth can show
> To inform a knowledge of desert, we know.*

These were the words, but the celestial harmony of the voices which sang them no tongue can describe: it took the ear of Ulysses with ravishment. He would have broken his bonds to rush after them; and threatened, wept, sued, entreated, commanded, crying out with tears and passionate imprecations, conjuring his men by all the ties of perils past which they had endured in common, by fellowship and love, and the authority which he retained among them, to let him loose; but at no rate would they obey him. And still the Sirens sang. Ulysses made signs, motions, gestures, promising mountains of gold if they would set him free; but their oars only moved faster. And still the Sirens sang. And still the more he adjured them to set him free, the faster with cords and ropes they

---

* To impart well-merited knowledge.

bound him; till they were quite out of hearing of the Sirens' notes, whose effect great Circe had so truly predicted. And well she might speak of them, for often she had joined her own enchanting voice to theirs, while she has sat in the flowery meads, mingled with the Sirens and the Water Nymphs, gathering their potent herbs and drugs of magic quality: their singing altogether has made the gods stoop, and "heaven drowsy with the harmony."

Escaped that peril, they had not sailed yet a hundred leagues farther, when they heard a roar afar off, which Ulysses knew to be the barking of Scylla's dogs, which surround her waist, and bark incessantly. Coming nearer they beheld a smoke ascend, with a horrid murmur, which arose from that other whirlpool, to which they made nigher approaches than to Scylla. Through the furious eddy, which is in that place, the ship stood still as a stone, for there was no man to lend his hand to an oar, the dismal roar of Scylla's dogs at a distance, and the nearer clamors of Charybdis, where everything made an echo, quite taking from them the power of exertion. Ulysses went up and down encouraging his men, one by one, giving them good words, telling them that they were in greater perils when they were blocked up in the Cyclop's cave, yet, Heaven assisting his counsels, he had delivered them out of that extremity. That he could not believe but they remembered it; and wished them to give the same trust to the same care which he had now for their welfare. That they must exert all the strength and wit which they had, and try if Jove would not grant them an escape even out of this peril. In particular, he cheered up the pilot who sat at the helm, and told him that he must show more firmness than other men, as he had more trust committed

to him, and had the sole management by his skill of the
vessel in which all their safeties were embarked. That a
rock lay hid within those boiling whirlpools which he saw,
on the outside of which he must steer, if he would avoid
his own destruction and the destruction of them all.

They heard him, and like men took to the oars; but
little knew what opposite danger, in shunning that rock,
they must be thrown upon. For Ulysses had concealed
from them the wounds, never to be healed, which Scylla
was to open: their terror would else have robbed them all
of all care to steer or move an oar, and have made them
hide under the hatches for fear of seeing her, where he and
they must have died an idle death. But even then he
forgot the precautions which Circe had given him to prevent harm to his person, who had willed him not to arm,
or show himself once to Scylla; but disdaining not to ven-
ture life for his brave companions, he could not contain,
but armed in all points, and taking a lance in either hand,
he went up to the fore-deck, and looked when Scylla
would appear.

She did not show herself as yet, and still the vessel
steered closer by her rock, as it sought to shun that other
more dreaded; for they saw how horribly Charybdis's
black throat drew into her all the whirling deep, which
she disgorged again, that all about her boiled like a kettle,
and the rock roared with troubled waters; which when
she supped in again, all the bottom turned up, and disclosed far under shore the swart sands naked, whose whole
stern sight frayed the startled blood from their faces, and
made Ulysses turn his to view the wonder of whirlpools.
Which when Scylla saw, from out her black den she darted

Swart: dark-colored, tawny.

out her six long necks, and swooped up as many of his friends: whose cries Ulysses heard, and saw them too late, with their heels turned up, and their hands thrown to him for succor, who had been their help in all extremities, but could not deliver them now; and he heard them shriek out, as she tore them, and to the last they continued to throw their hands out to him for sweet life. In all his sufferings he never had beheld a sight so full of miseries.

Escaped from Scylla and Charybdis, but with a diminished crew, Ulysses and the sad remains of his followers reached the Trinacrian shore. Here landing, he beheld oxen grazing of such surpassing size and beauty that, both from them and from the shape of the island (having three promontories jutting into the sea), he judged rightly that he was come to the Triangular island and the oxen of the Sun, of which Tiresias had forewarned him.

So great was his terror lest through his own fault, or that of his men, any violence or profanation should be offered to the holy oxen, that even then, tired as they were with the perils and fatigues of the day past, and unable to stir an oar, or use any exertion, and though night was fast coming on, he would have had them re-embark immediately, and make the best of their way from that dangerous station; but his men with one voice resolutely opposed it, and even the too cautious Eurylochus himself withstood the proposal; so much did the temptation of a little ease and refreshment (ease tenfold sweet after such labors) prevail over the sagest counsels, and the apprehension of certain evil outweigh the prospect of contingent danger. They expostulated that the nerves of Ulysses seemed to be made of steel, and his limbs not liable to lassitude like other men's; that waking or sleeping seemed indifferent to him;

but that they were men, not gods, and felt the common appetites for food and sleep. That in the night-time all the winds most destructive to ships are generated. That black night still required to be served with meat, and sleep, and quiet havens, and ease. That the best sacrifice to the sea was in the morning. With such sailor-like sayings and mutinous arguments, which the majority have always ready to justify disobedience to their betters, they forced Ulysses to comply with their requisition, and against his will to take up his night-quarters on shore. But he first exacted from them an oath that they would neither maim nor kill any of the cattle which they saw grazing, but content themselves with such food as Circe had stowed their vessel with when they parted from Æœa. This they man by man severally promised, imprecating the heaviest curses on whoever should break it; and mooring their bark within a creek, they went to supper, contenting themselves that night with such food as Circe had given them, not without many sad thoughts of their friends whom Scylla had devoured, the grief of which kept them great part of the night waking.

In the morning Ulysses urged them again to a religious observance of the oath that they had sworn, not in any case to attempt the blood of those fair herds which they saw grazing, but to content themselves with the ship's food; for the god who owned those cattle sees and hears all.

They faithfully obeyed, and remained in that good mind for a month, during which they were confined to that station by contrary winds, till all the wine and the bread were gone which they had brought with them. When their victuals were gone, necessity compelled them to stray in quest of whatever fish or fowl they could snare, which that coast did not yield in any great abundance. Then Ulysses prayed to all the gods that dwelt in bountiful heaven, that they would be pleased to yield them some means to stay their hunger without having recourse to profane and forbidden violations; but the ears of heaven seemed to be shut, or some god incensed plotted his ruin; for at midday, when he should chiefly have been vigilant and watchful to prevent mischief, a deep sleep fell upon the eyes of Ulysses, during which he lay totally insensible of all that passed in the world, and what his friends or what his enemies might do for his welfare or destruction. Then Eurylochus took his advantage. He was the man of most authority with them after Ulysses. He represented to them all the misery of their condition; how that every death is hateful and grievous to mortality, but that of all deaths famine is attended with the most painful, loathsome, and humiliating circumstances; that the subsistence which they could hope to draw from fowling or fishing was too precarious to be depended upon; that there did not seem to be any chance of the winds changing to favor their escape, but that they must inevitably stay there and perish, if they let an irrational superstition deter them from the means which nature offered to their hands; that Ulysses might be deceived in his belief that these oxen had any sacred qualities above other oxen; and even admitting that they were the property of the god of the Sun, as he said they were, the Sun did neither eat nor drink, and the gods were best served not by a scrupulous conscience, but by a thankful heart, which took freely what they as freely offered: with these and such like persuasions he prevailed on his half-famished and half-mutinous companions to begin the impious violation of their oath by the slaughter of seven of the fairest of these oxen which were grazing. Part they roasted and ate, and part they offered in sacrifice to the gods, particularly to Apollo, god of the Sun, vowing to build a temple to his godhead when they should arrive in Ithaca, and deck it with magnificent and numerous gifts. Vain men! and superstition worse than that which they so lately derided! to imagine that prospective penitence can excuse a present violation of duty, and that the pure natures of the heavenly powers will admit of compromise or dispensation for sin.

But to their feast they fell, dividing the roasted portions of the flesh, savory and pleasant meat to them, but a sad sight to the eyes, and a savor of death in the nostrils, of the waking Ulysses, who just woke in time to witness, but not soon enough to prevent, their rash and sacrilegious banquet. He had scarce time to ask what great mischief was this which they had done unto him; when behold, a prodigy! the ox-hides which they had stripped began to creep as if they had life; and the roasted flesh bellowed as the ox used to do when he was living. The hair of Ulysses stood up on end with affright at these omens; but his companions, like men whom the gods had infatuated to their destruction, persisted in their horrible banquet.

The Sun from his burning chariot saw how Ulysses's men had slain his oxen, and he cried to his father Jove, "Revenge me upon these impious men who have slain my oxen, which it did me good to look upon when I walked my heavenly round. In all my daily course I never saw such bright and beautiful creatures as those my oxen were." The father promised that ample retribution should be taken of those accursed men: which was fulfilled shortly after, when they took their leaves of the fatal island.

Six days they feasted in spite of the signs of heaven, and on the seventh, the wind changing, they set their sails and left the island; and their hearts were cheerful with the banquets they had held; all but the heart of Ulysses, which sank within him, as with wet eyes he beheld his friends, and gave them for lost, as men devoted to divine vengeance. Which soon overtook them; for they had not gone many leagues before a dreadful tempest arose, which burst their cables; down came their mast, crushing the skull of the pilot in its fall; off he fell from the stern into the water, and the bark wanting his management drove along at the wind's mercy; thunders roared, and terrible lightnings of Jove came down; first a bolt struck Eurylochus, then another, and then another, till all the crew were killed, and their bodies swam about like sea-mews; and the ship was split in pieces. Only Ulysses survived; and he had no hope of safety but in tying himself to the mast, where he sat riding upon the waves, like one that in no extremity would yield to fortune. Nine days was he floating about with all the motions of the sea, with no other support than the slender mast under him, till the tenth night cast him, all spent and weary with toil, upon the friendly shores of the island Ogygia.

Sea-mews: sea-gulls.   **Ogygia** (O-gy̆g′-I-a).

CHAPTER IV.

The Island of Calypso.—Immortality refused.

HENCEFORTH the adventures of the single Ulysses must be pursued. Of all those faithful partakers of his toil, who with him left Asia, laden with the spoils of Troy, now not one remains, but all a prey to the remorseless waves, and food for some great fish; their gallant navy reduced to one ship, and that finally swallowed up and lost. Where now are all their anxious thoughts of home? that perseverance with which they went through the severest sufferings and the hardest labors to which poor seafarers were ever exposed, that their toils at last might be crowned with the sight of their native shores and wives at Ithaca! Ulysses is now in the isle Ogygia, called the Delightful Island. The poor shipwrecked chief, the slave of all the elements, is once again raised by the caprice of fortune into a shadow of prosperity. He that was cast naked upon the shore, bereft of all his companions, has now a goddess to attend upon him, and his companions are the nymphs which never die. Who has not heard of Calypso? her grove crowned with alders and poplars; her grotto, against which the luxuriant vine laid forth his purple grapes; her ever new delights, crystal fountains, running brooks, meadows flowering with sweet balm-gentle and with violet; blue violets which like veins enamelled the smooth breasts of each fragrant mead! It were useless to describe over again what has been so well

Balm-gentle: balm-mint, a fragrant herb.

told already; or to relate those soft arts of courtship which the goddess used to detain Ulysses; the same in kind which she afterwards practised upon his less wary son, whom Minerva, in the shape of Mentor, hardly preserved from her snares, when they came to the Delightful Island together in search of the scarce departed Ulysses.

A memorable example of married love, and a worthy instance how dear to every good man his country is, was exhibited by Ulysses. If Circe loved him sincerely, Calypso loves him with tenfold more warmth and passion: she can deny him nothing, but his departure; she offers him everything, even to a participation of her immortality — if he will stay and share in her pleasures, he shall never die. But death with glory has greater charms for a mind heroic than a life that shall never die with shame; and when he pledged his vows to his Penelope, they had sworn to live and grow old together; and he would not survive her if he could, nor meanly share in immortality itself, from which she was excluded.

These thoughts kept him pensive and melancholy in the midst of pleasure. His heart was on the seas, making voyages to Ithaca. Twelve months had worn away, when Minerva from heaven saw her favorite, how he sat still pining on the sea-shores (his daily custom), wishing for a ship to carry him home. She (who is wisdom herself) was indignant that so wise and brave a man as Ulysses should be held in effeminate bondage by an unworthy goddess; and at her request her father Jove ordered Mercury to go down to the earth to command Calypso to dismiss her guest. The divine messenger tied fast to his feet his winged shoes, which bear him over land and seas, and took in his hand his golden rod, the ensign of his authority. Then wheeling in many an airy round, he stayed not till he alighted on the firm top of the mountain Pieria; thence he fetched a second circuit over the seas, kissing the waves in his flight with his feet, as light as any sea-mew fishing dips her wings, till he touched the isle Ogygia, and soared up from the blue sea to the grotto of the goddess to whom his errand was ordained.

His message struck a horror, checked by love, through all the faculties of Calypso. She replied to it, incensed: "You gods are insatiate, past all that live, in all things which you affect; which makes you so envious and grudging. It afflicts you to the heart when any goddess seeks the love of a mortal man in marriage. And now you envy me the possession of a wretched man whom tempests have cast upon my shores, making him lawfully mine; whose ship Jove rent in pieces with his hot thunderbolts, killing all his friends. Him I have preserved, loved, nourished; made him mine by protection, my creature; by every tie of gratitude, mine; have vowed to make him deathless like myself; him you will take from me. But I know your power, and that it is vain for me to resist. Tell your king that I obey his mandates."

With an ill grace Calypso promised to fulfil the commands of Jove; and, Mercury departing, she went to find Ulysses, where he sat outside the grotto, not knowing of the heavenly message, drowned in discontent, not seeing any human probability of his ever returning home.

She said to him: "Unhappy man, no longer afflict yourself with pining after your country, but build you a ship, with which you may return home, since it is the will of the gods; who, doubtless, as they are greater in

Pieria (Pi-c'-ri-a).

power than I, are greater in skill, and best can tell what is fittest for man. But I call the gods and my inward conscience to witness that I had no thought but what stood with thy safety, nor would have done or counselled anything against thy good. I persuaded thee to nothing which I should not have followed myself in thy extremity; for my mind is innocent and simple. O, if thou knewest what dreadful sufferings thou must yet endure before ever thou reachest thy native land, thou wouldest not esteem so hardly of a goddess's offer to share her immortality with thee; nor, for a few years' enjoyment of a perishing Penelope, refuse an imperishable and never-dying life with Calypso."

He replied: "Ever-honored, great Calypso, let it not displease thee, that I a mortal man desire to see and converse again with a wife that is mortal: human objects are best fitted to human infirmities. I well know how far in wisdom, in feature, in stature, proportion, beauty, in all the gifts of the mind, thou exceedest my Penelope: she is a mortal, and subject to decay; thou immortal, ever growing, yet never old; yet in her sight all my desires terminate, all my wishes — in the sight of her, and of my country earth. If any god, envious of my return, shall lay his dreadful hand upon me as I pass the seas, I submit; for the same powers have given me a mind not to sink under oppression. In wars and waves my sufferings have not been small."

She heard his pleaded reasons, and of force she must assent; so to her nymphs she gave in charge from her sacred woods to cut down timber, to make Ulysses a ship. They obeyed, though in a work unsuitable to their soft fingers, yet to obedience no sacrifice is hard; and Ulysses busily bestirred himself, laboring far more hard than they, as was fitting, till twenty tall trees, driest and fittest for timber, were felled. Then, like a skilful shipwright, he fell to joining the planks, using the plane, the axe, and the auger with such expedition that in four days' time a ship was made, complete with all her decks, hatches, sideboards, yards. Calypso added linen for the sails, and tackling; and when she was finished, she was a goodly vessel for a man to sail in, alone or in company, over the wide seas. By the fifth morning she was launched; and Ulysses, furnished with store of provisions, rich garments, and gold and silver, given him by Calypso, took a last leave of her and of her nymphs, and of the isle Ogygia which had so befriended him.

CHAPTER V.

The Tempest. — The Sea-bird's Gift. — The Escape by Swimming. — The Sleep in the Woods.

AT the stern of his solitary ship Ulysses sat, and steered right artfully. No sleep could seize his eyelids. He beheld the Pleiads, the Bear, which is by some called the Wain, that moves round about Orion, and keeps still above the ocean, and the slow-setting sign Bootes, which some name the Wagoner. Seventeen days he held his course, and on the eighteenth the coast of Phæacia was in sight. The figure of the land, as seen from the sea, was pretty and circular, and looked something like a shield.

Neptune, returning from visiting his favorite Æthiopians, from the mountains of the Solymi, descried Ulysses ploughing the waves, his domain. The sight of the man he so much hated for Polyphemus's sake, his son, whose eye Ulysses had put out, set the god's heart on fire; and snatching into his hand his horrid sea-sceptre, the trident of his power, he smote the air and the sea, and conjured up all his black storms, calling down night from the cope of heaven, and taking the earth into the sea, as it seemed, with clouds, through the darkness and indistinctness which prevailed; the billows rolling up before the fury of all the winds, that contended together in their mighty sport.

<small>Pleiads (Plei′-ăds *or* Plē-ads): the constellation of the Pleiades (Plei′-a-dēs *or* Plē′a-dēs).
Wain: a northern constellation, called also the "Great Dipper."
Bootes (Bŏ-ō′-tēs): a northern constellation near the Wain.
Phæacia (Phē-ă′-cĭ-a).</small>

Then the knees of Ulysses bent with fear, and then all his spirit was spent, and he wished that he had been among the number of his countrymen who fell before Troy, and had their funerals celebrated by all the Greeks, rather than to perish thus, where no man could mourn him or know him.

As he thought these melancholy thoughts, a huge wave took him and washed him overboard, ship and all upset amidst the billows, he struggling afar off, clinging to her stern broken off which he yet held, her mast cracking in two with the fury of that gust of mixed winds that struck it, sails and sail-yards fell into the deep, and he himself was long drowned under water, nor could get his head above, wave so met with wave, as if they strove which should depress him most; and the gorgeous garments given him by Calypso clung about him, and hindered his swimming; yet neither for this, nor for the overthrow of his ship, nor his own perilous condition, would he give up his drenched vessel; but, wrestling with Neptune, got at length hold of her again, and then sat in her hull, insulting over death, which he had escaped, and the salt waves which he gave the seas again to give to other men; his ship, striving to live, floated at random, cuffed from wave to wave, hurled to and fro by all the winds: now Boreas tossed it to Notus, Notus passed it to Eurus, and Eurus to the West Wind, who kept up the horrid tennis.

Them in their mad sport Ino Leucothea beheld — Ino Leucothea, now a sea-goddess, but once a mortal and the daughter of Cadmus; she with pity beheld Ulysses the mark of their fierce contention, and rising from the waves alighted on the ship, in shape like to the sea-bird which is

Leucothea (Leu-cŏth'-ĕ-a).

called a cormorant; and in her beak she held a wonderful girdle made of sea-weeds, which grow at the bottom of the ocean, which she dropped at his feet; and the bird spake to Ulysses, and counselled him not to trust any more to that fatal vessel against which god Neptune had levelled his furious wrath, nor to those ill-befriending garments which Calypso had given him, but to quit both it and them, and trust for his safety to swimming. "And here," said the seeming bird, "take this girdle and tie about your middle, which has virtue to protect the wearer at sea, and you shall safely reach the shore; but when you have landed, cast it far from you back into the sea." He did as the sea-bird instructed him; he stripped himself naked, and, fastening the wondrous girdle about his middle, cast himself into the seas to swim. The bird dived past his sight into the fathomless abyss of the ocean.

Two days and two nights he spent in struggling with the waves, though sore buffeted, and almost spent, never giving up himself for lost, such confidence he had in that charm which he wore about his middle, and in the words of that divine bird. But the third morning the winds grew calm and all the heavens were clear. Then he saw himself nigh land, which he knew to be the coast of the Phæacians, a people good to strangers and abounding in ships, by whose favor he doubted not that he should obtain a passage to his own country. And such joy he conceived in his heart as good sons have that esteem their father's life dear, when long sickness has held him down to his bed and wasted his body, and they see at length health return to the old man, with restored strength and spirits, in reward of their many prayers to the gods for his safety: so precious was the prospect of home-return to

Ulysses, that he might restore health to his country (his better parent), that had long languished as full of distempers in his absence. And then for his own safety's sake he had joy to see the shores, the woods, so nigh and within his grasp as they seemed, and he labored with all the might of hands and feet to reach with swimming that nigh-seeming land.

But when he approached near, a horrid sound of a huge sea beating against rocks informed him that here was no place for landing, nor any harbor for man's resort, but through the weeds and the foam which the sea belched up against the land he could dimly discover the rugged shore all bristled with flints, and all that part of the coast one impending rock that seemed impossible to climb, and the water all about so deep that not a sand was there for any tired foot to rest upon, and every moment he feared lest some wave more cruel than the rest should crush him against a cliff, rendering worse than vain all his landing; and should he swim to seek a more commodious haven farther on, he was fearful lest, weak and spent as he was, the winds would force him back a long way off into the main, where the terrible god Neptune, for wrath that he had so nearly escaped his power, having gotten him again into his domain, would send out some great whale (of which those seas breed a horrid number) to swallow him up alive; with such malignity he still pursued him.

While these thoughts distracted him with diversity of dangers, one bigger wave drove against a sharp rock his naked body, which it gashed and tore, and wanted little of breaking all his bones, so rude was the shock. But in this extremity she prompted him that never failed him at need. Minerva (who is wisdom itself) put it into his thoughts no longer to keep swimming off and on, as one dallying with danger, but boldly to force the shore that threatened him, and to hug the rock that had torn him so rudely; which with both hands he clasped, wrestling with extremity, till the rage of that billow which had driven him upon it was passed; but then again the rock drove back that wave so furiously that it reft him of his hold, sucking him with it in its return; and the sharp rock, his cruel friend, to which he clung for succor, rent the flesh so sore from his hands in parting that he fell off, and could sustain no longer; quite under water he fell, and, past the help of fate, there had the hapless Ulysses lost all portion that he had in this life, if Minerva had not prompted his wisdom in that peril to essay another course, and to explore some other shelter, ceasing to attempt that landing-place.

She guided his wearied and nigh-exhausted limbs to the mouth of the fair river Callicoe, which not far from thence disbursed its watery tribute to the ocean. Here the shores were easy and accessible, and the rocks, which rather adorned than defended its banks, so smooth that they seemed polished of purpose to invite the landing of our sea-wanderer, and to atone for the uncourteous treatment which those less hospitable cliffs had afforded him. And the god of the river, as if in pity, stayed his current, and smoothed his waters, to make his landing more easy; for sacred to the ever-living deities of the fresh waters, be they mountain-stream, river, or lake, is the cry of erring mortals that seek their aid, by reason that, being inland-bred, they partake more of the gentle humanities of our nature than those marine deities whom Neptune trains up in tempests in the unpitying recesses of his salt abyss.

Callicoe (Căl-lik′-ŏ-ĕ).

So by the favor of the river's god Ulysses crept to land half-drowned; both his knees faltering, his strong hands falling down through weakness from the excessive toils he had endured, his cheeks and nostrils flowing with froth of the sea-brine, much of which he had swallowed in that conflict, voice and breath spent, down he sank as in death. Dead weary he was. It seemed that the sea had soaked through his heart, and the pains he felt in all his veins were little less than those which one feels that has endured the torture of the rack. But when his spirits came a little to themselves, and his recollection by degrees began to return, he rose up, and unloosing from his waist the girdle or charm which that divine bird had given him, and remembering the charge which he had received with it, he flung it far from him into the river. Back it swam with the course of the ebbing stream till it reached the sea, where the fair hands of Ino Leucothea received it to keep it as a pledge of safety to any future shipwrecked mariner that, like Ulysses, should wander in those perilous waves.

Then he kissed the humble earth in token of safety, and on he went by the side of that pleasant river, till he came where a thicker shade of rushes that grew on its banks seemed to point out the place where he might rest his sea-wearied limbs. And here a fresh perplexity divided his mind, whether he should pass the night, which was coming on, in that place, where, though he feared no other enemies, the damps and frosts of the chill sea-air in that exposed situation might be death to him in his weak state; or whether he had better climb the next hill, and pierce the depth of some shady wood, in which he might find a warm and sheltered though insecure repose, subject to the approach of any wild beast that roamed that way. Best did this last course appear to him, though with some danger, as that which was more honorable and savored more of strife and self-exertion than to perish without a struggle the passive victim of cold and the elements.

So he bent his course to the nearest woods, where, entering in, he found a thicket, mostly of wild olives and such low trees; yet growing so intertwined and knit together that the moist wind had not leave to play through their branches, nor the sun's scorching beams to pierce their recesses, nor any shower to beat through, they grew so thick, and as it were folded each in the other; here creeping in, he made his bed of the leaves which were beginning to fall, of which was such abundance that two or three men might have spread them ample coverings, such as might shield them from the winter's rage, though the air breathed steel and blew as it would burst. Here creeping in, he heaped up store of leaves all about him, as a man would billets upon a winter fire, and lay down in the midst. Rich seed of virtue lying hid in poor leaves! Here Minerva soon gave him sound sleep; and here all his long toils past seemed to be concluded and shut up within the little sphere of his refreshed and closed eyelids.

CHAPTER VI.

The Princess Nausicaa. — The Washing. — The Game with the Ball. — The Court of Phæacia and King Alcinous.

MEANTIME Minerva, designing an interview between the king's daughter of that country and Ulysses when he should awake, went by night to the palace of king Alcinous, and stood at the bedside of the princess Nausicaa in the shape of one of her favorite attendants, and thus addressed the sleeping princess;

"Nausicaa, why do you lie sleeping here, and never bestow a thought upon your bridal ornaments, of which you have many and beautiful, laid up in your wardrobe against the day of your marriage, which cannot be far distant; when you shall have need of all, not only to deck your own person, but to give away in presents to the virgins that honoring you shall attend you to the temple? Your reputation stands much upon the timely care of these things; these things are they which fill father and reverend mother with delight. Let us arise betimes to wash your fair vestments of linen and silks in the river; and request your sire to lend you mules and a coach, for your wardrobe is heavy, and the place where we must wash is distant, and besides it fits not a great princess like you to go so far on foot."

So saying, she went away, and Nausicaa awoke, full

Nausicaa (Nau-sĭk′-ā-ā).   **Alcinous** (Al-cĭn′-ŏ-us).

of pleasing thoughts of her marriage, which the dream had told her was not far distant; and as soon as it was dawn she arose and dressed herself, and went to find her parents.

The queen her mother was already up, and seated among her maids, spinning at her wheel, as the fashion was in those primitive times, when great ladies did not disdain housewifery: and the king her father was preparing to go abroad at that early hour to council with his grave senate.

"My father," she said, "will you not order mules and a coach to be got ready, that I may go and wash, I and my maids, at the cisterns that stand without the city?"

"What washing does my daughter speak of?" said Alcinous.

"Mine and my brothers' garments," she replied, "that have contracted soil by this time with lying by so long in the wardrobe. Five sons have you that are my brothers; two of them are married, and three are bachelors; these last it concerns to have their garments neat and unsoiled; it may advance their fortunes in marriage: and who but I their sister should have a care of these things? You yourself, my father, have need of the whitest apparel when you go, as now, to the council."

She used this plea, modestly dissembling her care of her own nuptials to her father; who was not displeased at this instance of his daughter's discretion; for a seasonable care about marriage may be permitted to a young maiden, provided it be accompanied with modesty and dutiful submission to her parents in the choice of her future husband; and there was no fear of

Nausicaa choosing wrongly or improperly, for she was as wise as she was beautiful, and the best in all Phæacia were suitors to her for her love. So Alcinous readily gave consent that she should go, ordering mules and a coach to be prepared. And Nausicaa brought from her chamber all her vestments, and laid them up in the coach, and her mother placed bread and wine in the coach, and oil in a golden cruse, to soften the bright skins of Nausicaa and her maids when they came out of the river.

Nausicaa, making her maids get up into the coach with her, lashed the mules, till they brought her to the cisterns which stood a little on the outside of the town, and were supplied with water from the river Callicoe.

There her attendants unyoked the mules, took out the clothes, and steeped them in the cisterns, washing them in several waters, and afterwards treading them clean with their feet, venturing wagers who should have done soonest and cleanest, and using many pretty pastimes to beguile their labors as young maids use, while the princess looked on. When they had laid their clothes to dry, they fell to playing again, and Nausicaa joined them in a game with the ball, which is used in that country, which is performed by tossing the ball from hand to hand with great expedition, she who begins the pastime singing a song. It chanced that the princess, whose turn it became to toss the ball, sent it so far from its mark that it fell beyond into one of the cisterns of the river; at which the whole company, in merry consternation, set up a shriek so loud as waked the sleeping Ulysses, who was taking his rest after his long toils in the woods not far distant from the place where these young maids had come to wash.

At the sound of female voices Ulysses crept forth from his retirement, making himself a covering with boughs and leaves as well as he could to shroud his nakedness. The sudden appearance of his weather-beaten and almost naked form so frightened the maidens that they scudded away into the woods and all about to hide themselves, only Minerva (who had brought about this interview to admirable purposes, by seemingly accidental means) put courage into the breast of Nausicaa, and she stayed where she was, and resolved to know what manner of man he was, and what was the occasion of his strange coming to them.

He not venturing (for delicacy) to approach and clasp her knees, as suppliants should, but standing far off, addressed this speech to the young princess:

"Before I presume rudely to press my petitions, I should first ask whether I am addressing a mortal woman, or one of the goddesses. If a goddess, you seem to me to be likest to Diana, the chaste huntress, the daughter of Jove. Like hers are your lineaments, your stature, your features, and air divine."

She making answer that she was no goddess, but a mortal maid, he continued:

"If a woman, thrice blessed are both the authors of your birth, thrice blessed are your brothers, who even to rapture must have joy in your perfections, to see you grown so like a young tree, and so graceful. But most blessed of all that breathe is he that has the gift to engage your young neck in the yoke of marriage. I never saw that man that was worthy of you. I never saw man or woman that at all parts equalled you. Lately at Delos (where I touched) I saw a young palm which grew beside

Diana (Dī-an'-a *or* Dī-ā'-na).

Apollo's temple; it exceeded all the trees which ever I beheld for straightness and beauty: I can compare you only to that. A stupor past admiration strikes me, joined with fear, which keeps me back from approaching you, to embrace your knees. Nor is it strange; for one of freshest and firmest spirit would falter, approaching near to so bright an object: but I am one whom a cruel habit of calamity has prepared to receive strong impressions. Twenty days the unrelenting seas have tossed me up and down coming from Ogygia, and at length cast me shipwrecked last night upon your coast. I have seen no man or woman since I landed but yourself. All that I crave is clothes, which you may spare me, and to be shown the way to some neighboring town. The gods, who have care of strangers, will requite you for these courtesies."

She, admiring to hear such complimentary words proceed out of the mouth of one whose outside looked so rough and unpromising, made answer: "Stranger, I discern neither sloth nor folly in you, and yet I see that you are poor and wretched: from which I gather that neither wisdom nor industry can secure felicity; only Jove bestows it upon whomsoever he pleases. He perhaps has reduced you to this plight. However, since your wanderings have brought you so near to our city, it lies in our duty to supply your wants. Clothes and what else a human hand should give to one so suppliant, and so tamed with calamity, you shall not want. We will show you our city and tell you the name of our people. This is the land of the Phæacians, of which my father, Alcinous, is king.

Then calling her attendants, who had dispersed on the

Admiring: wondering.

first sight of Ulysses, she rebuked them for their fear, and said: "This man is no Cyclop, nor monster of sea or land, that you should fear him; but he seems manly, staid, and discreet, and though decayed in his outward appearance, yet he has the mind's riches, wit and fortitude, in abundance. Show him the cisterns, where he may wash him from the sea-weeds and foam that hang about him, and let him have garments that fit him, out of those which we have brought with us to the cisterns."

Ulysses, retiring a little out of sight, cleansed him in the cisterns from the soil and impurities with which the rocks and waves had covered all his body, and clothing himself with befitting raiment, which the princess's attendants had given him, he presented himself in more worthy shape to Nausicaa. She admired to see what a comely personage he was, now he was dressed in all parts; she thought him some king or hero: and secretly wished that the gods would be pleased to give her such a husband.

Then causing her attendants to yoke her mules, and lay up the vestments, which the sun's heat had sufficiently dried, in the coach, she ascended with her maids, and drove off to the palace; bidding Ulysses, as she departed, keep an eye upon the coach, and to follow it on foot at some distance: which she did, because if she had suffered him to ride in the coach with her, it might have subjected her to some misconstructions of the common people, who are always ready to vilify and censure their betters, and to suspect that charity is not always pure charity, but that love or some sinister intention lies hid under its disguise. So discreet and attentive to appearance in all her actions was this admirable princess.

Ulysses as he entered the city wondered to see its magnificence, its markets, buildings, temples; its walls and ramparts; its trade, and resort of men; its harbors for shipping, which is the strength of the Phæacian state. But when he approached the palace, and beheld its riches, the proportion of its architecture, its avenues, gardens, statues, fountains, he stood rapt in admiration, and almost forgot his own condition in surveying the flourishing estate of others; but recollecting himself, he passed on boldly into the inner apartment, where the king and queen were sitting at dinner with their peers, Nausicaa having prepared them for his approach.

To them humbly kneeling, he made it his request that, since fortune had cast him naked upon their shores, they would take him into their protection, and grant him a conveyance by one of the ships of which their great Phæacian state had such good store, to carry him to his own country. Having delivered his request, to grace it with more humility he went and sat himself down upon the hearth among the ashes, as the custom was in those days when any would make a petition to the throne.

He seemed a petitioner of so great state and of so superior a deportment that Alcinous himself arose to do him honor, and causing him to leave that abject station which he had assumed, placed him next to his throne, upon a chair of state, and thus he spake to his peers:

"Lords and councillors of Phæacia, ye see this man, who he is we know not, that is come to us in the guise of a petitioner: he seems no mean one; but whoever he is, it is fit, since the gods have cast him upon our protection, that we grant him the rites of hospitality while he stays with us, and at his departure a ship well manned to convey so worthy a personage as he seems to be, in a manner suitable to his rank, to his own country."

This counsel the peers with one consent approved; and wine and meat being set before Ulysses, he ate and drank, and gave the gods thanks who had stirred up the royal bounty of Alcinous to aid him in that extremity. But not as yet did he reveal to the king and queen who he was, or whence he had come; only in brief terms he related his being cast upon their shores, his sleep in the woods, and his meeting with the princess Nausicaa, whose generosity, mingled with discretion, filled her parents with delight, as Ulysses in eloquent phrases adorned and commended her virtues. But Alcinous, humanely considering that the troubles which his guest had undergone required rest, as well as refreshment by food, dismissed him early in the evening to his chamber; where in a magnificent apartment Ulysses found a smoother bed, but not a sounder repose, than he had enjoyed the night before, sleeping upon leaves which he had scraped together in his necessity.

CHAPTER VII.

The Songs of Demodocus. — The Convoy Home. — The Mariners transformed to Stone. — The Young Shepherd.

WHEN it was daylight, Alcinous caused it to be proclaimed by the heralds about the town that there was come to the palace a stranger, shipwrecked on their coast, that in mien and person resembled a god; and inviting all the chief people of the city to come and do honor to the stranger.

The palace was quickly filled with guests, old and young, for whose cheer, and to grace Ulysses more, Alcinous made a kingly feast with banquetings and music. Then, Ulysses being seated at a table next the king and queen, in all men's view, after they had feasted Alcinous ordered Demodocus, the court-singer, to be called to sing some song of the deeds of heroes, to charm the ear of his guest. Demodocus came and reached his harp, where it hung between two pillars of silver; and then the blind singer, to whom, in recompense of his lost sight, the muses had given an inward discernment, a soul and a voice to excite the hearts of men and gods to delight, began in grave and solemn strains to sing the glories of men highliest famed. He chose a poem whose subject was The Stern Strife stirred up between Ulysses and Great Achilles, as at a banquet sacred to the gods, in dreadful language, they expressed their difference; while Agamemnon sat

Demodocus (De-mod′-o-cus).

rejoiced in soul to hear those Grecians jar; for the oracle in Pytho had told him that the period of their wars in Troy should then be, when the kings of Greece, anxious to arrive at the wished conclusion, should fall to strife, and contend which must end the war, force or stratagem.

This brave contention he expressed so to the life, in the very words which they both used in the quarrel, as brought tears into the eyes of Ulysses at the remembrance of past passages of his life, and he held his large purple weed before his face to conceal it. Then craving a cup of wine, he poured it out in secret libation to the gods, who had put into the mind of Demodocus unknowingly to do him so much honor. But when the moving poet began to tell of other occurrences where Ulysses had been present, the memory of his brave followers who had been with him in all difficulties, now swallowed up and lost in the ocean, and of those kings that had fought with him at Troy, some of whom were dead, some exiles like himself, forced itself so strongly upon his mind that forgetful where he was he sobbed outright with passion: which yet he restrained, but not so cunningly but Alcinous perceived it, and without taking notice of it to Ulysses, privately gave signs that Demodocus should cease from his singing.

Next followed dancing in the Phæacian fashion, when they would show respect to their guests; which was succeeded by trials of skill, games of strength, running, racing, hurling of the quoit, mock fights, hurling of the javelin, shooting with the bow: in some of which Ulysses modestly challenging his entertainers, performed such feats of strength and prowess as gave the admiring Phæacians fresh reason to imagine that he was either some god, or hero of the race of the gods.

Weed: an outer garment.

These solemn shows and pageants in honor of his guest king Alcinous continued for the space of many days, as if he could never be weary of showing courtesies to so worthy a stranger. In all this time he never asked him his name, nor sought to know more of him than he of his own accord disclosed; till on a day as they were seated feasting, after the feast was ended, Demodocus being called, as was the custom, to sing some grave matter, sang how Ulysses, on that night when Troy was fired, made dreadful proof of his valor, maintaining singly a combat against the whole household of Deiphobus, to which the divine expresser gave both act and passion, and breathed such a fire into Ulysses's deeds that it inspired old death with life in the lively expressing of slaughters, and rendered life so sweet and passionate in the hearers that all who heard felt it fleet from them in the narration: which made Ulysses even pity his own slaughterous deeds, and feel touches of remorse, to see how song can revive a dead man from the grave, yet no way can it defend a living man from death; and in imagination he underwent some part of death's horrors, and felt in his living body a taste of those dying pangs which he had dealt to others; that with the strong conceit, tears (the true interpreters of unutterable emotion) stood in his eyes.

Which king Alcinous noting, and that this was now the second time that he had perceived him to be moved at the mention of events touching the Trojan wars, he took occasion to ask whether his guest had lost any friend or kinsman at Troy, that Demodocus's singing had brought into his mind. Then Ulysses, drying the tears with his cloak, and observing that the eyes of all the company were

Deiphobus (Dē-Iph′-o-bus).   **Conceit**: fancy.

upon him, desirous to give them satisfaction in what he could, and thinking this a fit time to reveal his true name and destination, spake as follows:

"The courtesies which ye all have shown me, and in particular yourself and princely daughter, O king Alcinous, demand from me that I should no longer keep you in ignorance of what or who I am; for to reserve any secret from you, who have with such openness of friendship embraced my love, would argue either a pusillanimous or an ungrateful mind in me. Know, then, that I am that *Ulysses*, of whom I perceive ye have heard something; who heretofore have filled the world with the renown of my policies. I am he by whose counsels, if Fame is to be believed at all, more than by the united valor of all the Grecians, Troy fell. I am that unhappy man whom the heavens and angry gods have conspired to keep an exile on the seas, wandering to seek my home, which still flies from me. The land which I am in quest of is Ithaca; in whose ports some ship belonging to your navigation-famed Phæacian state may haply at some time have found a refuge from tempests. If ever you have experienced such kindness, requite it now, by granting to me, who am the king of that land, a passport to that land."

Admiration seized all the court of Alcinous, to behold in their presence one of the number of those heroes who fought at Troy, whose divine story had been made known to them by songs and poems, but of the truth they had little known, or rather they had hitherto accounted those heroic exploits as fictions and exaggerations of poets; but having seen and made proof of the real Ulysses, they began to take those supposed inventions to be real verities, and the tale of Troy to be as true as it was delightful.

Then king Alcinous made answer: "Thrice fortunate ought we to esteem our lot, in having seen and conversed with a man of whom report hath spoken so loudly, but, as it seems, nothing beyond the truth. Though we could desire no felicity greater than to have you always among us, renowned Ulysses, yet your desire having been expressed so often and so deeply to return home, we can deny you nothing, though to our own loss. Our kingdom of Phæacia, as you know, is chiefly rich in shipping. In all parts of the world, where there are navigable seas, or ships can pass, our vessels will be found. You cannot name a coast to which they do not resort. Every rock and every quicksand is known to them that lurks in the vast deep. They pass a bird in flight; and with such unerring certainty they make to their destination that some have said that they have no need of pilot or rudder, but that they move instinctively, self-directed, and know the minds of their voyagers. Thus much, that you may not fear to trust yourself in one of our Phæacian ships. To-morrow, if you please, you shall launch forth. To-day spend with us in feasting, who never can do enough when the gods send such visitors."

Ulysses acknowledged king Alcinous's bounty; and while these two royal personages stood interchanging courteous expressions, the heart of the princess Nausicaa was overcome: she had been gazing attentively upon her father's guest as he delivered his speech; but when he came to that part where he declared himself to be Ulysses, she blessed herself and her fortune that in relieving a poor shipwrecked mariner, as he seemed no better, she had conferred a kindness on so divine a hero as he proved; and scarce waiting till her father had done speaking, with a cheerful countenance she addressed Ulysses, bidding him be cheerful, and when he returned home, as by her father's means she trusted he would shortly, sometimes to remember to whom he owed his life, and who met him in the woods by the river Callicoe.

"Fair flower of Phæacia," he replied, "so may all the gods bless me with the strife of joys in that desired day, whenever I shall see it, as I shall always acknowledge to be indebted to your fair hand for the gift of life which I enjoy, and all the blessings which shall follow upon my home-return. The gods give thee, Nausicaa, a princely husband; and from you two spring blessings to this state." So prayed Ulysses, his heart overflowing with admiration and grateful recollections of king Alcinous's daughter.

Then at the king's request he gave them a brief relation of all the adventures that had befallen him since he launched forth from Troy; during which the princess Nausicaa took great delight (as ladies are commonly taken with these kind of travellers' stories) to hear of the monster Polyphemus, of the men that devour each other in Læstrygonia, of the enchantress Circe, of Scylla, and the rest; to which she listened with a breathless attention, letting fall a shower of tears from her fair eyes every now and then, when Ulysses told of some more than usual distressful passage in his travels; and all the rest of his auditors, if they had before entertained a high respect for their guest, now felt their veneration increased tenfold, when they learned from his own mouth what perils, what sufferance, what endurance, of evils beyond man's strength to support, this much-sustaining, almost heavenly man, by the greatness of his mind, and by his invincible courage, had struggled through.

The night was far spent before Ulysses had ended his narrative, and with wishful glances he cast his eyes towards the eastern parts, which the sun had begun to flecker with his first red; for on the morrow Alcinous had promised that a bark should be in readiness to convoy him to Ithaca.

In the morning a vessel well manned and appointed was waiting for him; into which the king and queen heaped presents of gold and silver, massy plate, apparel, armor, and whatsoever things of cost or rarity they judged would be most acceptable to their guest; and the sails being set, Ulysses, embarking with expressions of regret, took his leave of his royal entertainers, of the fair princess (who had been his first friend), and of the peers of Phæacia; who crowding down to the beach to have the last sight of their illustrious visitant, beheld the gallant ship with all her canvas spread, bounding and curveting over the waves, like a horse proud of his rider, or as if she knew that in her capacious hold's rich freightage she bore Ulysses.

He whose life past had been a series of disquiets, in seas among rude waves, in battles amongst ruder foes, now slept securely, forgetting all; his eye-lids bound in such deep sleep as only yielded to death; and when they reached the nearest Ithacan port by the next morning, he was still asleep. The mariners, not willing to awake him, landed him softly, and laid him in a cave at the foot of an olive-tree, which made a shady recess in that narrow harbor, the haunt of almost none but the sea-nymphs, which are called Naiads; few ships before this Phæacian vessel having put into that haven, by reason of the difficulty and narrowness of the entrance. Here leaving him asleep, and disposing in safe places near him the presents with which king Alcinous had dismissed him, they departed for Phæacia; where these wretched mariners never again set foot; but just as they arrived, and thought to salute their country earth, in sight of their city's turrets, and in open view of their friends, who from the harbor with shouts greeted their return, their vessel and all the mariners which were in her were turned to stone, and stood transformed and fixed in sight of the whole Phæacian city, where it yet stands, by Neptune's vindictive wrath; who resented thus highly the contempt which those Phæacians had shown in convoying home a man whom the god had destined to destruction. Whence it comes to pass that the Phæacians at this day will at no price be induced to lend their ships to strangers, or to become the carriers for other nations, so highly do they still dread the displeasure of their sea-god, while they see that terrible monument ever in sight.

When Ulysses awoke, which was not till some time after the mariners had departed, he did not at first know his country again, either that long absence had made it strange, or that Minerva (which was more likely) had cast a cloud about his eyes, that he should have greater pleasure hereafter in discovering his mistake; but like a man suddenly awaking in some desert isle, to which his sea-mates have transported him in his sleep, he looked around, and discerning no known objects, he cast his hands to heaven for pity, and complained of those ruthless men who had beguiled him with a promise of conveying him home to his country, and perfidiously left him to perish in an unknown land. But then the rich presents of gold and silver given him by Alcinous, which he saw carefully laid up in secure places near him, staggered him: which seemed not like the act of wrongful or unjust men, such as turn pirates for gain, or land helpless passengers in remote coasts to possess themselves of their goods.

While he remained in this suspense, there came up to him a young shepherd, clad in the finer sort of apparel, such as kings' sons wore in those days when princes did not disdain to tend sheep, who, accosting him, was saluted again by Ulysses, who asked him what country that was on which he had been just landed, and whether it were part of a continent, or an island. The young shepherd made show of wonder, to hear any one ask the name of that land; as country people are apt to esteem those for mainly ignorant and barbarous who do not know the names of places which are familiar to *them*, though perhaps they who ask have had no opportunities of knowing, and may have come from far countries.

"I had thought," said he, "that all people knew our land. It is rocky and barren, to be sure; but well enough: it feeds a goat or an ox well; it is not wanting either in wine or in wheat; it has good springs of water, some fair rivers; and wood enough, as you may see: it is called Ithaca."

Ulysses was joyed enough to find himself in his own country; but so prudently he carried his joy, that, dissembling his true name and quality, he pretended to the shepherd that he was only some foreigner, who, by stress of weather, had put into that port; and framed on the sudden a story to make it plausible, how he had come from Crete in a ship of Phæacia; when the young shepherd, laughing, and taking Ulysses's hand in both his, said to him: "He must be cunning, I find, who thinks to overreach you. What, cannot you quit your wiles and your subtleties, now that you are in a state of security? must the first word with which you salute your native earth be an untruth? and think you that you are unknown?"

Ulysses looked again; and he saw, not a shepherd, but a beautiful woman, whom he immediately knew to be the goddess Minerva, that in the wars of Troy had frequently vouchsafed her sight to him; and had been with him since in perils, saving him unseen.

"Let not my ignorance offend thee, great Minerva," he cried, " or move thy displeasure, that in that shape I knew thee not; since the skill of discerning of deitiés is not attainable by wit or study, but hard to be hit by the wisest of mortals. To know thee truly through all thy changes is only given to those whom thou art pleased to grace. To all men thou takest all likenesses. All men in their wits think that they know thee, and that they have thee. Thou art wisdom itself. But a semblance of thee, which is false wisdom, often is taken for thee; so thy counterfeit view appears to many, but thy true presence to few: those are they which, loving thee above all, are inspired with light from thee to know thee. But this I surely know, that all the time the sons of Greece waged war against Troy, I was sundry times graced with thy appearance; but since, I have never been able to set eyes upon thee till now; but have wandered at my own discretion, to myself a blind guide, erring up and down the world, wanting thee."

Then Minerva cleared his eyes, and he knew the ground on which he stood to be Ithaca, and that cave to be the same which the people of Ithaca had in former times made sacred to the sea-nymphs, and where he himself had done sacrifices to them a thousand times; and full in his view stood Mount Nerytus with all his woods: so that now he knew for a certainty that he was arrived in his own country, and with the delight which he felt he could not forbear stooping down and kissing the soil.

Nerytus (Ner'-y̆-tus).

CHAPTER VIII.

The Change from a King to a Beggar.—Eumæus and the Herdsman.
—Telemachus.

NOT long did Minerva suffer him to indulge vain transports; but briefly recounting to him the events which had taken place in Ithaca during his absence, she showed him that his way to his wife and throne did not lie so open, but that before he were reinstated in the secure possession of them he must encounter many difficulties. His palace, wanting its king, was become the resort of insolent and imperious men, the chief nobility of Ithaca and of the neighboring isles, who, in the confidence of Ulysses being dead, came as suitors to Penelope. The queen (it was true) continued single, but was little better than a state-prisoner in the power of these men, who, under a pretence of waiting her decision, occupied the king's house rather as owners than guests, lording and domineering at their pleasure, profaning the palace and wasting the royal substance with their feasts and mad riots. Moreover, the goddess told him how, fearing the attempts of these lawless men upon the person of his young son Telemachus, she herself had put it into the heart of the prince to go and seek his father in far countries; how in the shape of Mentor she had born him company in his long search; which, though failing, as she meant it should fail, in its first object, had yet had this effect, that through

Eumæus (Eu-mē'-ŭs).   Telemachus (Tĕ-lĕm'-ȧ-kus).

hardships he had learned endurance, through experience he had gathered wisdom, and wherever his footsteps had been he had left such memorials of his worth as the fame of Ulysses's son was already blown throughout the world. That it was now not many days since Telemachus had arrived in the island, to the great joy of the queen his mother, who had thought him dead, by reason of his long absence, and had begun to mourn for him with a grief equal to that which she endured for Ulysses: the goddess herself having so ordered the course of his adventures that the time of his return should correspond with the return of Ulysses, that they might together concert measures how to repress the power and insolence of those wicked suitors. This the goddess told him; but of the particulars of his son's adventures, of his having been detained in the Delightful Island, which his father had so lately left, of Calypso and her nymphs, and the many strange occurrences which may be read with profit and delight in the history of the prince's adventures, she forbore to tell him as yet, as judging that he would hear them with greater pleasure from the lips of his son, when he should have him in an hour of stillness and safety, when their work should be done, and none of their enemies left alive to trouble them.

Then they sat down, the goddess and Ulysses, at the foot of a wild olive-tree, consulting how they might with safety bring about his restoration. And when Ulysses revolved in his mind how that his enemies were a multitude, and he single, he began to despond, and he said, "I shall die an ill death like Agamemnon; in the threshold of my own house I shall perish, like that unfortunate monarch, slain by some one of my wife's suitors." But then again calling to mind his ancient courage, he secretly wished that Minerva would but breathe such a spirit into his bosom as she inflamed him with in the hour of Troy's destruction, that he might encounter with three hundred of those impudent suitors at once, and strew the pavements of his beautiful palace with their blood and brains.

And Minerva knew his thoughts, and she said, "I will be strongly with thee, if thou fail not to do thy part. And for a sign between us that I will perform my promise, and for a token on thy part of obedience, I must change thee, that thy person may not be known of men."

Then Ulysses bowed his head to receive the divine impression, and Minerva by her great power changed his person so that it might not be known. She changed him to appearance into a very old man, yet such a one as by his limbs and gait seemed to have been some considerable person in his time, and to retain yet some remains of his once prodigious strength. Also, instead of those rich robes in which king Alcinous had clothed him, she threw over his limbs such old and tattered rags as wandering beggars usually wear. A staff supported his steps, and a scrip hung to his back, such as travelling mendicants use to hold the scraps which are given to them at rich men's doors. So from a king he became a beggar, as wise Tiresias had predicted to him in the shades.

To complete his humiliation, and to prove his obedience by suffering, she next directed him in this beggarly attire to go and present himself to his old herdsman Eumæus, who had the care of his swine and his cattle, and had been a faithful steward to him all the time of his absence. Then strictly charging Ulysses that he should reveal himself to no man, but to his own son, whom she would send to him when she saw occasion, the goddess went her way.

The transformed Ulysses bent his course to the cottage of the herdsman, and, entering in at the front court, the dogs, of which Eumæus kept many fierce ones for the protection of the cattle, flew with open mouths upon him, as those ignoble animals have oftentimes an antipathy to the sight of anything like a beggar, and would have rent him in pieces with their teeth, if Ulysses had not had the prudence to let fall his staff, which had chiefly provoked their fury, and sat himself down in a careless fashion upon the ground; but for all that, some serious hurt had certainly been done to him, so raging the dogs were, had not the herdsman, whom the barking of the dogs had fetched out of the house, with shouting and with throwing of stones repressed them.

He said, when he saw Ulysses, "Old father, how near you were to being torn in pieces by these rude dogs! I should never have forgiven myself, if through neglect of mine any hurt had happened to you. But Heaven has given me so many cares to my portion that I might well be excused for not attending to everything: while here I lie grieving and mourning for the absence of that majesty which once ruled here, and am forced to fatten his swine and his cattle for food to evil men, who hate him and who wish his death; when he perhaps strays up and down the world, and has not wherewith to appease hunger, if indeed he yet lives (which is a question) and enjoys the cheerful light of the sun." This he said, little thinking that he of whom he spoke now stood before him, and that in that uncouth disguise and beggarly obscurity was present the hidden majesty of Ulysses.

Then he had his guest into the house, and set meat and drink before him; and Ulysses said, "May Jove and all the other gods requite you for the kind speeches and hospitable usage which you have shown me!"

Eumæus made answer, "My poor guest, if one in much worse plight than yourself had arrived here, it were a shame to such scanty means as I have if I had let him depart without entertaining him to the best of my ability. Poor men, and such as have no houses of their own, are by Jove himself recommended to our care. But the cheer which we, that are servants to other men, have to bestow is but sorry at most, yet freely and lovingly I give it you. Indeed, there once ruled here a man, whose return the gods have set their faces against, who, if he had been suffered to reign in peace and grow old among us, would have been kind to me and mine. But he is gone; and for his sake would to God that the whole posterity of Helen might perish with her, since in her quarrel so many worthies have perished! But such as your fare is, eat it, and be welcome — such lean beasts as are food for poor herdsmen. The fattest go to feed the voracious stomachs of the queen's suitors. Shame on their unworthiness! there is no day in which two or three of the noblest of the herd are not slain to support their feasts and their surfeits."

Ulysses gave good ear to his words; and as he ate his meat, he even tore it and rent it with his teeth, for mere vexation that his fat cattle should be slain to glut the appetites of those godless suitors. And he said, "What chief or what ruler is this, that thou commendest so highly, and sayest that he perished at Troy? I am but a stranger in these parts. It may be I have heard of some such in my long travels."

Eumæus answered, "Old father, never any one of all the strangers that have come to our coast with news of Ulysses being alive could gain credit with the queen or her son yet. These travellers, to get raiment or a meal, will not stick to invent any lie. Truth is not the commodity they deal in. Never did the queen get anything of them but lies. She receives all that come graciously, hears their stories, inquires all she can, but all ends in tears and dissatisfaction. But in God's name, old father, if you have got a tale, make the most on't, it may gain you a cloak or a coat from somebody to keep you warm; but for him who is the subject of it, dogs and vultures long since have torn him limb from limb, or some great fish at sea has devoured him, or he lieth with no better monument upon his bones than the sea-sand. But for me, past all the race of men were tears created; for I never shall find so kind a royal master more; not if my father or my mother could come again and visit me from the tomb, would my eyes be so blessed, as they should be with the sight of him again, coming as from the dead. In his last rest my soul shall love him. He is not here, nor do I name him as a flatterer, but because I am thankful for his love and care which he had to me a poor man; and if I knew surely that he were past all shores that the sun shines upon, I would invoke him as a deified being."

For this saying of Eumæus the waters stood in Ulysses's eyes, and he said, "My friend, to say and to affirm positively that he cannot be alive is to give too much license to incredulity. For, not to speak at random, but with as much solemnity as an oath comes to, I say to you that Ulysses shall return; and whenever that day shall be, then shall you give to me a cloak and a coat; but till then, I will not receive so much as a thread of a garment, but rather go naked; for no less than the gates of hell do I hate that man whom poverty can force to tell an untruth. Be Jove then witness to my words, that this very year, nay, ere this month be fully ended, your eyes shall behold Ulysses, dealing vengeance in his own palace upon the wrongers of his wife and his son."

To give the better credence to his words, he amused Eumæus with a forged story of his life; feigning of himself that he was a Cretan born, and one that went with Idomeneus to the wars of Troy. Also he said that he knew Ulysses, and related various passages which he alleged to have happened betwixt Ulysses and himself, which were either true in the main, as having really happened between Ulysses and some other person, or were so like to truth, as corresponding with the known character and actions of Ulysses, that Eumæus's incredulity was not a little shaken. Among other things he asserted that he had lately been entertained in the court of Thesprotia, where the king's son of the country had told him that Ulysses had been there but just before him, and was gone upon a voyage to the oracle of Jove in Dodona, whence he should shortly return, and a ship would be ready by the bounty of the Thesprotians to convoy him straight to Ithaca. "And in token that what I tell you is true," said Ulysses, "if your king come not within the period which I have named, you shall have leave to give your servants commandment to take my old carcass, and throw it headlong from some steep rock into the sea, that poor

Idomeneus (Ī-dŏm′-e-neus).
Oracle: a declaration of the will of the gods, particularly their answer to a direct inquiry made at one of their temples or groves.

men, taking example by me, may fear to lie." But Eumæus made answer that that should be small satisfaction or pleasure to him.

So while they sat discoursing in this manner, supper was served in, and the servants of the herdsman, who had been out all day in the fields, came in to supper, and took their seats at the fire, for the night was bitter and frosty. After supper, Ulysses, who had well eaten and drunken, and was refreshed with the herdsman's good cheer, was resolved to try whether his host's hospitality would extend to the lending him a good warm mantle or rug to cover him in the night season; and framing an artful tale for the purpose, in a merry mood, filling a cup of Greek wine, he thus began:

"I will tell you a story of your king Ulysses and myself. If there is ever a time when a man may have leave to tell his own stories, it is when he has drunken a little too much. Strong liquor driveth the fool, and moves even the heart of the wise, moves and impels him to sing and to dance, and break forth in pleasant laughters, and perchance to prefer a speech too which were better kept in. When the heart is open, the tongue will be stirring. But you shall hear. We led our powers to ambush once under the walls of Troy."

The herdsmen crowded about him eager to hear anything which related to their king Ulysses and the wars of Troy, and thus he went on:

"I remember, Ulysses and Menelaus had the direction of that enterprise, and they were pleased to join me with them in the command. I was at that time in some repute among men, though fortune has played me a trick since, as you may perceive. But I was somebody in those times, and could do something. Be that as it may, a bitter freezing night it was, such a night as this, the air cut like steel, and the sleet gathered on our shields like crystal. There was some twenty of us, that lay close crouched down among the reeds and bulrushes that grew in the moat that goes round the city. The rest of us made tolerable shift, for every man had been careful to bring with him a good cloak or mantle to wrap over his armor and keep himself warm; but I, as it chanced, had left my cloak behind me, as not expecting that the night would prove so cold, or rather, I believe, because I had at that time a brave suit of new armor on, which, being a soldier, and having some of the soldier's vice about me — *vanity* — I was not willing should be hidden under a cloak; but I paid for my indiscretion with my sufferings, for with the inclement night, and the wet of the ditch in which we lay, I was well-nigh frozen to death; and when I could endure no longer, I jogged Ulysses who was next to me, and had a nimble ear, and made known my case to him, assuring him that I must inevitably perish. He answered in a low whisper, 'Hush, lest any Greek should hear you, and take notice of your softness.' Not a word more he said, but showed as if he had no pity for the plight I was in. But he was as considerate as he was brave; and even then, as he lay with his head reposing upon his hand, he was meditating how to relieve me, without exposing my weakness to the soldiers. At last, raising up his head, he made as if he had been asleep, and said, 'Friends, I have been warned in a dream to send to the fleet to king Agamemnon for a supply, to recruit our numbers, for we are not sufficient for this enterprise;' and they believing him, one Thoas was despatched on that errand, who departing, for more speed, as Ulysses had foreseen, left his upper garment behind him, a good warm mantle, to which I succeeded, and by the help of it got through the night with credit. This shift Ulysses made for one in need, and would to heaven that I had now that strength in my limbs which made me in those days to be accounted fit to be a leader under Ulysses! I should not then want the loan of a cloak or a mantle, to wrap about me and shield my old limbs from the night air."

The tale pleased the herdsmen; and Eumæus, who more than all the rest was gratified to hear tales of Ulysses, true or false, said that for his story he deserved a mantle, and a night's lodging, which he should have; and he spread for him a bed of goat and sheep skins by the fire; and the seeming beggar, who was indeed the true Ulysses, lay down and slept under that poor roof, in that abject disguise to which the will of Minerva had subjected him.

When morning was come, Ulysses made offer to depart, as if he were not willing to burden his host's hospitality any longer, but said that he would go and try the humanity of the townsfolk, if any there would bestow upon him a bit of bread or a cup of drink. Perhaps the queen's suitors (he said), out of their full feasts, would bestow a scrap on him; for he could wait at table, if need were, and play the nimble serving-man; he could fetch wood (he said) or build a fire, prepare roast meat or boiled, mix the wine with water, or do any of those offices which recommended poor men like him to services in great men's houses.

"Alas! poor guest," said Eumæus, "you know not what you speak. What should so poor and old a man as you do at the suitors' tables? Their light minds are not given to such grave servitors. They must have youths, richly tricked out in flowing vests, with curled hair, like so many of Jove's cupbearers, to fill out the wine to them as they sit at table, and to shift their trenchers. Their gorged insolence would but despise and make a mock at thy age. Stay here. Perhaps the queen, or Telemachus, hearing of thy arrival, may send to thee of their bounty."

As he spoke these words, the steps of one crossing the front court were heard, and a noise of the dogs fawning and leaping about as for joy; by which token Eumæus guessed that it was the prince, who, hearing of a traveller being arrived at Eumæus's cottage that brought tidings of his father, was come to search the truth; and Eumæus said, "It is the tread of Telemachus, the son of king Ulysses." Before he could well speak the words, the prince was at the door, whom Ulysses rising to receive, Telemachus would not suffer that so aged a man, as he appeared, should rise to do respect to him, but he courteously and reverently took him by the hand, and inclined his head to him, as if he had surely known that it was his father indeed; but Ulysses covered his eyes with his hands, that he might not show the waters which stood in them. And Telemachus said, "Is this the man who can tell us tidings of the king my father?"

"He brags himself to be a Cretan born," said Eumæus, "and that he has been a soldier and a traveller, but whether he speak the truth or not he alone can tell. But whatsoever he has been, what he is now is apparent. Such as he appears, I give him to you; do what you will with him; his boast at present is that he is at the very best a supplicant."

Trenchers : wooden-plates.

"Be what he may," said Telemachus, "I accept him at your hands. But where I should bestow him I know not, seeing that in the palace his age would not exempt him from the scorn and contempt which my mother's suitors in their light minds would be sure to fling upon him: a mercy if he escaped without blows; for they are a company of evil men, whose profession is wrongs and violence."

Ulysses answered: "Since it is free for any man to speak in presence of your greatness, I must say that my heart puts on a wolfish inclination to tear and to devour, hearing your speech, that these suitors should with such injustice rage, where you should have the rule solely. What should the cause be? do you wilfully give way to their ill manners? or has your government been such as has procured ill-will towards you from your people? or do you mistrust your kinsfolk and friends in such sort as without trial to decline their aid? A man's kindred are they that he might trust to when extremities run high."

Telemachus replied: "The kindred of Ulysses are few. I have no brothers to assist me in the strife. But the suitors are powerful in kindred and friends. The house of old Arcesius has had this fate from the heavens, that from old it still has been supplied with single heirs. To Arcesius, Laertes only was born, from Laertes descended only Ulysses, from Ulysses I alone have sprung, whom he left so young that from me never comfort arose to him. But the end of all rests in the hands of the gods."

Then Eumæus departing to see to some necessary business of his herds, Minerva took a woman's shape, and stood in the entry of the door, and was seen by Ulysses, but by his son she was not seen, for the presences of the gods are invisi-

Arcesius (Ar-cē'-sĭ-us).

ble save to those to whom they will to reveal themselves. Nevertheless, the dogs which were about the door saw the goddess, and durst not bark, but went crouching and licking of the dust for fear. And giving signs to Ulysses that the time was now come in which he should make himself known to his son, by her great power she changed back his shape into the same which it was before she transformed him; and Telemachus, who saw the change, but nothing of the manner by which it was effected, only he saw the appearance of a king in the vigor of his age where but just now he had seen a worn and decrepit beggar, was struck with fear, and said, "Some god has done this house this honor," and he turned away his eyes, and would have worshipped. But his father permitted not, but said, " Look better at me; I am no deity, why put you upon me the reputation of godhead? I am no more but thy father: I am even he; I am that Ulysses by reason of whose absence thy youth has been exposed to such wrongs from injurious men." Then kissed he his son, nor could any longer refrain those tears which he had held under such mighty restraint before, though they would ever be forcing themselves out in spite of him; but now, as if their sluices had burst, they came out like rivers, pouring upon the warm cheeks of his son. Nor yet by all these violent arguments could Telemachus be persuaded to believe that it was his father, but he said some deity had taken that shape to mock him; for he affirmed that it was not in the power of any man, who is sustained by mortal food, to change his shape so in a moment from age to youth: for, "but now," said he, " you were all wrinkles, and were old, and now you look as the gods are pictured."

His father replied: "Admire, but fear not, and know

me to be at all parts substantially thy father, who in the inner powers of his mind, and the unseen workings of a father's love to thee, answers to his outward shape and pretence! There shall no more Ulysseses come here. I am he that after twenty years' absence, and suffering a world of ill, have recovered at last the sight of my country earth. It was the will of Minerva that I should be changed as you saw me. She put me thus together; she puts together or takes to pieces whom she pleases. It is in the law of her free power to do it: sometimes to show her favorites under a cloud, and poor, and again to restore to them their ornaments. The gods raise and throw down men with ease."

Then Telemachus could hold out no longer, but he gave way now to a full belief and persuasion, of that which for joy at first he could not credit, that it was indeed his true and very father that stood before him; and they embraced, and mingled their tears.

Then said Ulysses, "Tell me who these suitors are, what are their numbers, and how stands the queen thy mother affected to them?"

"She bears them still in expectation," said Telemachus, "which she never means to fulfil, that she will accept the hand of some one of them in second nuptials. For she fears to displease them by an absolute refusal. So from day to day she lingers them on with hope, which they are content to bear the deferring of, while they have entertainment at free cost in our palace."

Then said Ulysses, "Reckon up their numbers that we may know their strength and ours, if we having none but ourselves may hope to prevail against them."

"O father," he replied, "I have ofttimes heard of your

fame for wisdom, and of the great strength of your arm, but the venturous mind which your speeches now indicate moves me even to amazement: for in nowise can it consist with wisdom or a sound mind that two should try their strengths against a host. Nor five, or ten, or twice ten strong are these suitors, but many more by much; from Dulichium came there fifty and two, they and their servants; twice twelve crossed the seas hither from Samos; from Zacynthus twice ten; of our native Ithacans, men of chief note, are twelve who aspire to the hand and crown of Penelope; .and all these under one strong roof — a fearful odds against two! My father, there is need of caution, lest the cup which your great mind so thirsts to taste of vengeance prove bitter to yourself in the drinking. And therefore it were well that we should bethink us of some one who might assist us in this undertaking."

"Thinkest thou," said his father, "if we had Minerva and the king of skies to be our friends, would their sufficiences make strong our part; or must we look out for some further aid yet?"

"They you speak of are above the clouds," said Telemachus, "and are sound aids indeed; as powers that not only exceed human, but bear the chiefest sway among the gods themselves."

Then Ulysses gave directions to his son to go and mingle with the suitors, and in nowise to impart his secret to any, not even to the queen his mother, but to hold himself in readiness, and to have his weapons and his good armor in preparation. And he charged him that when he himself should come to the palace, as he meant to follow shortly after, and present himself in his beggar's likeness to the

Dulichium (Dū-lĭk′-ĭ-um).

suitors, that whatever he should see which might grieve his heart, with what foul usage and contumelious language soever the suitors should receive his father, coming in that shape, though they should strike and drag him by the heels along the floors, that he should not stir nor make offer to oppose them, further than by mild words to expostulate with them, until Minerva from heaven should give the sign which should be the prelude to their destruction. And Telemachus, promising to obey his instructions, departed; and the shape of Ulysses fell to what it had been before, and he became to all outward appearance a beggar, in base and beggarly attire.

CHAPTER IX.

The Queen's Suitors. — The Battle of the Beggars. — The Armor taken down. — The Meeting with Penelope.

FROM the house of Eumæus the seeming beggar took his way, leaning on his staff, till he reached the palace, entering in at the hall where the suitors sat at meat. They in the pride of their feasting began to break their jests in mirthful manner, when they saw one looking so poor and so aged approach. He, who expected no better entertainment, was nothing moved at their behavior, but, as became the character which he had assumed, in a suppliant posture crept by turns to every suitor, and held out his hands for some charity, with such a natural and beggar-resembling grace that he might seem to have practised begging all his life; yet there was a sort of dignity in his most abject stoopings, that whoever had seen him would have said, If it had pleased Heaven that this poor man had been born a king, he would gracefully have filled a throne. And some pitied him, and some gave him alms, as their present humors inclined them, but the greater part reviled him, and bade him begone, as one that spoiled their feast; for the presence of misery has this power with it, that, while it stays, it can dash and overturn the mirth even of those who feel no pity or wish to relieve it: nature bearing this witness of herself in the hearts of the most obdurate.

Now Telemachus sat at meat with the suitors, and knew that it was the king his father who in that shape begged an alms; and when his father came and presented himself before him in turn, as he had done to the suitors one by one, he gave him of his own meat which he had in his dish, and of his own cup to drink. And the suitors were past measure offended to see a pitiful beggar, as they esteemed him, to be so choicely regarded by the prince.

Then Antinous, who was a great lord, and of chief note among the suitors, said, "Prince Telemachus does ill to encourage these wandering beggars, who go from place to place, affirming that they have been some considerable persons in their time, filling the ears of such as hearken to them with lies, and pressing with their bold feet into kings' palaces. This is some saucy vagabond, some travelling Egyptian."

"I see," said Ulysses, "that a poor man should get but little at your board; scarce should he get salt from your hands, if he brought his own meat."

Lord Antinous, indignant to be answered with such sharpness by a supposed beggar, snatched up a stool, with which he smote Ulysses where the neck and shoulders join. This usage moved not Ulysses; but in his great heart he meditated deep evils to come upon them all, which for a time must be kept close, and he went and sat himself down in the door-way to eat of that which was given him; and he said, "For life or possessions a man will fight, but for his appetite this man smites. If a poor man has any god to take his part, my lord Antinous shall not live to be the queen's husband."

Then Antinous raged highly, and threatened to drag him by the heels, and to rend his rags about his ears, if he spoke another word.

But the other suitors did in nowise approve of the harsh

language, nor of the blow which Antinous had dealt; and some of them said, "Who knows but one of the deities goes about hid under that poor disguise? for in the likeness of poor pilgrims the gods have many times descended to try the dispositions of men, whether they be humane or impious." While these things passed, Telemachus sat and observed all, but held his peace, remembering the instructions of his father. But secretly he waited for the sign which Minerva was to send from heaven.

That day there followed Ulysses to the court one of the common sort of beggars, Irus by name, one that had received alms beforetime of the suitors, and was their ordinary sport, when they were inclined (as that day) to give way to mirth, to see him eat and drink; for he had the appetite of six men, and was of huge stature and proportions of body; yet had in him no spirit nor courage of a man. This man, thinking to curry favor with the suitors, and recommend himself especially to such a great lord as Antinous was, began to revile and scorn Ulysses, putting foul language upon him, and fairly challenging him to fight with the fist. But Ulysses, deeming his railings to be nothing more than jealousy and that envious disposition which beggars commonly manifest to brothers in their trade, mildly besought him not to trouble him, but to enjoy that portion which the liberality of their entertainers gave him, as he did quietly; seeing that, of their bounty, there was sufficient for all.

But Irus, thinking that this forbearance in Ulysses was nothing more than a sign of fear, so much the more highly stormed, and bellowed, and provoked him to fight; and by this time the quarrel had attracted the notice of the suitors, who with loud laughters and shouting egged on the dispute, and lord Antinous swore by all the gods it should be a battle, and that in that hall the strife should be determined. To this the rest of the suitors with violent clamors acceded, and a circle was made for the combatants, and a fat goat was proposed as the victor's prize, as at the Olympic or the Pythian games. Then Ulysses, seeing no remedy, or being not unwilling that the suitors should behold some proof of that strength which ere long in their own persons they were to taste of, stripped himself, and prepared for the combat. But first, he demanded that he should have fair play shown him, that none in that assembly should aid his opponent, or take part against him, for, being an old man, they might easily crush him with their strengths. And Telemachus passed his word that no foul play should be shown him, but that each combatant should be left to his own unassisted strengths, and to this he made Antinous and the rest of the suitors swear.

But when Ulysses had laid aside his garments, and was bare to the waist, all the beholders admired at the goodly sight of his large shoulders, being of such exquisite shape and whiteness, and at his great and brawny bosom, and the youthful strength which seemed to remain in a man thought so old; and they said, What limbs and what sinews he has! and coward fear seized on the mind of that great vast beggar, and he dropped his threats, and his big words, and would have fled, but lord Antinous stayed him, and threatened him that if he declined the combat, he would put him in a ship, and land him on the shores where king Echetus reigned, the roughest tyrant which at that time the world contained, and who had that antipathy to rascal beggars, such as he, that when any landed on his coast he would crop

Echetus (Ĕk′-ē-tus).

their ears and noses and give them to the dogs to tear. So Irus, in whom fear of king Echetus prevailed above the fear of Ulysses, addressed himself to fight. But Ulysses, provoked to be engaged in so odious a strife with a fellow of his base conditions, and loathing longer to be made a spectacle to entertain the eyes of his foes, with one blow, which he struck him beneath the ear, so shattered the teeth and jawbone of this soon baffled coward that he laid him sprawling in the dust, with small stomach or ability to renew the contest. Then raising him on his feet, he led him bleeding and sputtering to the door, and put his staff into his hand, and bade him go use his command upon dogs and swine, but not presume himself to be lord of the guests another time, nor of the beggary!

The suitors applauded in their vain minds the issue of the contest, and rioted in mirth at the expense of poor Irus, who, they vowed, should be forthwith embarked, and sent to king Echetus; and they bestowed thanks on Ulysses for ridding the court of that unsavory morsel, as they called him; but in their inward souls they would not have cared if Irus had been victor, and Ulysses had taken the foil, but it was mirth to them to see the beggars fight. In such pastimes and light entertainments the day wore away.

When evening was come, the suitors betook themselves to music and dancing. And Ulysses leaned his back against a pillar from which certain lamps hung which gave light to the dancers, and he made show of watching the dancers, but very different thoughts were in his head. And as he stood near the lamps, the light fell upon his head, which was thin of hair and bald, as an old man's. And Eurymachus, a suitor, taking occasion from some

Eurymachus (Eu-rўm′-å-kus).

words which were spoken before, scoffed, and said, "Now I know for a certainty that some god lurks under the poor and beggarly appearance of this man, for, as he stands by the lamps, his sleek head throws beams around it, like as it were a glory." And another said, "He passes his time, too, not much unlike the gods, lazily living exempt from labor, taking offerings of men." "I warrant," said Eurymachus again, "he could not raise a fence or dig a ditch for his livelihood, if a man would hire him to work in a garden."

"I wish," said Ulysses, "that you, who speak this, and myself were to be tried at any taskwork: that I had a good crooked scythe put in my hand, that was sharp and strong, and you such another, where the grass grew longest, to be up by daybreak, mowing the meadows till the sun went down, not tasting of food till we had finished; or that we were set to plough four acres in one day of good glebe land, to see whose furrows were evenest and cleanest; or that we might have one wrestling-bout together; or that in our right hands a good steel-headed lance were placed, to try whose blows fell heaviest and thickest upon the adversary's head-piece. I would cause you such work as you should have small reason to reproach me with being slack at work. But you would do well to spare me this reproach, and to save your strength till the owner of this house shall return, till the day when Ulysses shall return, when returning he shall enter upon his birthright."

This was a galling speech to those suitors, to whom Ulysses's return was indeed the thing which they most dreaded; and a sudden fear fell upon their souls, as if

Glebe: land that has not been ploughed.

they were sensible of the real presence of that man who
did indeed stand amongst them, but not in that form
as they might know him; and Eurymachus, incensed,
snatched a massy cup which stood on a table near and
hurled it at the head of the supposed beggar, and but narrowly missed the hitting of him; and all the suitors rose,
as at once, to thrust him out of the hall, which they said
his beggarly presence and his rude speeches had profaned.
But Telemachus cried to them to forbear, and not to presume to lay hands upon a wretched man to whom he had
promised protection. He asked if they were mad, to mix
such abhorred uproar with his feasts. He bade them take
their food and their wine, to sit up or to go to bed at their
free pleasures, so long as he should give license to that
freedom; but why should they abuse his banquet, or let
the words which a poor beggar spake have power to move
their spleens so fiercely?

They bit their lips and frowned for anger to be checked
so by a youth; nevertheless for that time they had the
grace to abstain, either for shame, or that Minerva had
infused into them a terror of Ulysses's son.

So that day's feast was concluded without bloodshed,
and the suitors, tired with their sports, departed severally
each man to his apartment. Only Ulysses and Telemachus remained. And now Telemachus, by his father's
direction, went and brought down into the hall armor and
lances from the armory; for Ulysses said, "On the morrow we shall have need of them." And moreover he said,
"If any one shall ask why you have taken them down,
say it is to clean them and scour them from the rust which
they have gathered since the owner of this house went to
Troy." And as Telemachus stood by the armor, the

lights were all gone out, and it was pitch dark, and the armor gave out glistering beams as of fire, and he said to his father, "The pillars of the house are on fire." And his father said, "It is the gods who sit above the stars, and have power to make the night as light as the day." And he took it for a good omen. And Telemachus fell to cleaning and sharpening of the lances.

Now Ulysses had not seen his wife Penelope in all the time since his return; for the queen did not care to mingle with the suitors at their banquets, but, as became one that had been Ulysses's wife, kept much in private, spinning, and doing her excellent housewiferies among her maids, in the remote apartments of the palace. Only upon solemn days she would come down and show herself to the suitors. And Ulysses was filled with a longing desire to see his wife again, whom for twenty years he had not beheld, and he softly stole through the known passages of his beautiful house, till he came where the maids were lighting the queen through a stately gallery that led to the chamber where she slept. And when the maids saw Ulysses, they said, "It is the beggar who came to the court to-day, about whom all that uproar was stirred up in the hall: what does he here?" But Penelope gave commandment that he should be brought before her, for she said, "It may be that he has travelled, and has heard something concerning Ulysses."

Then was Ulysses right glad to hear himself named by his queen, to find himself in nowise forgotten, nor her great love towards him decayed in all that time that he had been away. And he stood before his queen, and she knew him not to be Ulysses, but supposed that he had been some poor traveller. And she asked him of what country he was.

He told her (as he had before told Eumæus) that he was a Cretan born, and, however poor and cast down he now seemed, no less a man than brother to Idomeneus, who was grandson to king Minos; and though he now wanted bread, he had once had it in his power to feast Ulysses. Then he feigned how Ulysses, sailing for Troy, was forced by stress of weather to put his fleet in at a port of Crete, where for twelve days he was his guest, and entertained by him with all befitting guest-rites. And he described the very garments which Ulysses had on, by which Penelope knew he had seen her lord.

In this manner Ulysses told his wife many tales of himself, at most but painting, but painting so near to the life that the feeling of that which she took in at her ears became so strong that the kindly tears ran down her fair cheeks, while she thought upon her lord, dead as she thought him, and heavily mourned the loss of him whom she missed, whom she could not find, though in very deed he stood so near her.

Ulysses was moved to see her weep, but he kept his own eyes dry as iron or horn in their lids, putting a bridle upon his strong passion, that it should not issue to sight.

Then told he how he had lately been at the court of Thresprotia, and what he had learned concerning Ulysses there, in order as he had delivered to Eumæus; and Penelope was wont to believe that there might be a possibility of Ulysses being alive, and she said, "I dreamed a dream this morning. Methought I had twenty household fowl which did eat wheat steeped in water from my hand, and there came suddenly from the clouds a crook-beaked hawk, who soused on them and killed them all, trussing their

Trussing: pulling, *i.e.*, wringing.

necks; then took his flight back up to the clouds. And in my dream methought that I wept and made great moan for my fowls, and for the destruction which the hawk had made; and my maids came about me to comfort me. And in the height of my griefs the hawk came back, and lighting upon the beam of my chamber, he said to me in a man's voice, which sounded strangely even in my dream, to hear a hawk to speak: 'Be of good cheer,' he said, 'O daughter of Icarius! for this is no dream which thou hast seen, but that which shall happen to thee indeed. Those household fowl, which thou lamentest so without reason, are the suitors who devour thy substance, even as thou sawest the fowl eat from thy hand; and the hawk is thy husband, who is coming to give death to the suitors.' And I awoke, and went to see to my fowls if they were alive, whom I found eating wheat from their troughs, all well and safe as before my dream."

Then said Ulysses, "This dream can endure no other interpretation than that which the hawk gave to it, who is your lord, and who is coming quickly to effect all that his words told you."

"Your words," she said, "my old guest, are so sweet that would you sit and please me with your speech, my ears would never let my eyes close their spheres for very joy of your discourse; but none that is merely mortal can live without the death of sleep, so the gods who are without death themselves have ordained it, to keep the memory of our mortality in our minds, while we experience that, as much as we live, we die every day; in which consideration I will ascend my bed, which I have nightly watered with my tears since he that was my joy departed for that bad city" — she so speaking because she could not bring her lips to name the name of Troy so much hated. So for that night they parted, Penelope to her bed, and Ulysses to his son, and to the armor and the lances in the hall, where they sat up all night, cleaning and watching by the armor.

CHAPTER X.

The Madness from Above. — The Bow of Ulysses. — The Slaughter. — The Conclusion.

WHEN daylight appeared, a tumultuous concourse of suitors again filled the hall; and some wondered, and some enquired what meant that glittering store of armor and lances which lay in heaps by the entry of the door; and to all that asked Telemachus made reply that he had caused them to be taken down to cleanse them of the rust and of the stain which they had contracted by lying so long unused, even ever since his father went to Troy; and with that answer their minds were easily satisfied. So to their feasting and vain rioting again they fell. Ulysses, by Telemachus's order, had a seat and a mess assigned to him in the doorway, and he had his eye ever on the lances. And it moved gall in some of the great ones there present to have their feast still dulled with the society of that wretched beggar as they deemed him, and they reviled and spurned at him with their feet. Only there was one Philœtius, who had something a better nature than the rest, that spake kindly to him, and had his age in respect. He, coming up to Ulysses, took him by the hand with a kind of fear, as if touched exceedingly with imagination of his great worth, and said thus to him, "Hail! father stranger! my brows have sweat to see the injuries which you have received, and my eyes have broke

Philœtius (Phi-lē'-tĭ-us).

forth in tears, when I have only thought that such being oftentimes the lot of worthiest men, to this plight Ulysses may be reduced, and that he now may wander from place to place as you do; for such who are compelled by need to range here and there, and have no firm home to fix their feet upon, God keeps them in this earth as under water; so are they kept down and depressed. And a dark thread is sometimes spun in the fates of kings."

At this bare likening of the beggar to Ulysses, Minerva from heaven made the suitors for foolish joy to go mad, and roused them to such a laughter as would never stop — they laughed without power of ceasing, their eyes stood full of tears for violent joys; but fears and horrible misgivings succeeded; and one among them stood up and prophesied: "Ah, wretches!" he said, "what madness from heaven has seized you, that you can laugh? see you not that your meat drops blood? a night, like the night of death, wraps you about; you shriek without knowing it; your eyes thrust forth tears; the fixed walls, and the beam that bears the whole house up, fall blood; ghosts choke up the entry; full is the hall with apparitions of murdered men; under your feet is hell; the sun falls from heaven, and it is midnight at noon." But like men whom the gods had infatuated to their destruction, they mocked at his fears, and Eurymachus said, "This man is surely mad; conduct him forth into the market-place, set him in the light, for he dreams that 'tis night within the house."

But Theoclymenus (for that was the prophet's name), whom Minerva had graced with a prophetic spirit, that he foreseeing might avoid the destruction which awaited them, answered and said: "Eurymachus, I will not re-

Theoclymenus (Thĕ-ŏ-clym'-ĕ-nus).

quire a guide of thee, for I have eyes and ears, the use of both my feet, and a sane mind within me, and with these I will go forth of the doors, because I know the imminent evils which await all you that stay, by reason of this poor guest who is a favorite with all the gods." So saying, he turned his back upon those inhospitable men, and went away home, and never returned to the palace.

These words which he spoke were not unheard by Telemachus, who kept still his eye upon his father, expecting fervently when he would give the sign which was to precede the slaughter of the suitors.

They, dreaming of no such thing, fell sweetly to their dinner, as joying in the great store of banquet which was heaped in full tables about them; but there reigned not a bitterer banquet planet in all heaven than that which hung over them this day by secret destination of Minerva.

There was a bow which Ulysses left when he went to Troy. It had lain by since that time, out of use and unstrung, for no man had strength to draw that bow, save Ulysses. So it had remained, as a monument of the great strength of its master. This bow, with the quiver of arrows belonging thereto, Telemachus had brought down from the armory on the last night along with the lances: and now Minerva, intending to do Ulysses an honor, put it into the mind of Telemachus to propose to the suitors to try who was strongest to draw that bow; and he promised that to the man who should be able to draw that bow his mother should be given in marriage — Ulysses's wife the prize to him who should bend the bow of Ulysses.

There was great strife and emulation stirred up among the suitors at those words of the prince Telemachus. And to grace her son's words, and to confirm the promise which he had made, Penelope came and showed herself that day to the suitors; and Minerva made her that she appeared never so comely in their sight as that day, and they were inflamed with the beholding of so much beauty, proposed as the price of so great manhood; and they cried out that if all those heroes who sailed to Colchis for the rich purchase of the golden-fleeced ram had seen earth's richer prize, Penelope, they would not have made their voyage, but would have vowed their valors and their lives to her, for she was at all parts faultless.

And she said, "The gods have taken my beauty from me, since my lord went for Troy." But Telemachus willed his mother to depart and not be present at that contest; for he said, "It may be, some rougher strife shall chance of this than may be expedient for a woman to witness." And she retired, she and her maids, and left the hall.

Then the bow was brought into the midst, and a mark was set up by prince Telemachus; and lord Antinous, as the chief among the suitors, had the first offer; and he took the bow, and, fitting an arrow to the string, he strove to bend it, but not with all his might and main could he once draw together the ends of that tough bow; and when he found how vain a thing it was to endeavor to draw Ulysses's bow, he desisted, blushing for shame and for mere anger. Then Eurymachus adventured, but with no better success; but as it had torn the hands of Antinous, so did the bow tear and strain his hands, and marred his delicate fingers, yet could he not once stir the string. Then called he to the attendants to bring fat and unctuous matter, which melting at the fire, he dipped the bow there-

Colchis (Cŏl'-kis).

in, thinking to supple it and make it more pliable; but not with all the helps of art could he succeed in making it to move. After him others essayed their strength, but not any one of them, or of the rest of those aspiring suitors, had any better luck; yet not the meanest of them there but thought himself well worthy of Ulysses's wife, though to shoot with Ulysses's bow the completest champion among them was by proof found too feeble.

Then Ulysses prayed that he might have leave to try; and immediately a clamor was raised among the suitors, because of his petition, and they scorned and swelled with rage at his presumption, and that a beggar should seek to contend in a game of such noble mastery. But Telemachus ordered that the bow should be given him, and that he should have leave to try, since they had failed; "for," he said, "the bow is mine, to give or to withhold;" and none durst gainsay the prince.

Then Ulysses gave a sign to his son, and he commanded the doors of the hall to be made fast, and all wondered at his words, but none could divine the cause. And Ulysses took the bow into his hands, and before he essayed to bend it, he surveyed it at all parts, to see whether, by long lying by, it had contracted any stiffness which hindered the drawing; and as he was busied in the curious surveying of his bow, some of the suitors mocked him, and said, "Past doubt this man is a right cunning archer, and knows his craft well. See how he turns it over and over, and looks into it, as if he could see through the wood." And others said, "We wish some one would tell out gold into our laps but for so long a time as he shall be in drawing of that string." But when he had spent some little time in making proof of the bow, and had found it to be in good plight, like as a harper in tuning of his harp draws out a string, with such ease or much more did Ulysses draw to the head the string of his own tough bow, and in letting of it go, it twanged with such a shrill noise as a swallow makes when it sings through the air; which so much amazed the suitors that their colors came and went, and the skies gave out a noise of thunder, which at heart cheered Ulysses, for he knew that now his long labors by the disposal of the Fates drew to an end. Then fitted he an arrow to the bow, and drawing it to the head, he sent it right to the mark which the prince had set up. Which done, he said to Telemachus, "You have got no disgrace yet by your guest, for I have struck the mark I shot at, and gave myself no such trouble in teasing the bow with fat and fire as these men did, but have made proof that my strength is not impaired, nor my age so weak and contemptible as these were pleased to think it. But come, the day going down calls us to supper, after which succeed poem and harp, and all delights which use to crown princely banquetings."

So saying, he beckoned to his son, who straight girt his sword to his side, and took one of the lances (of which there lay great store from the armory) in his hand, and armed at all points advanced towards his father.

The upper rags which Ulysses wore fell from his shoulder, and his own kingly likeness returned, when he rushed to the great hall door with bow and quiver full of shafts, which down at his feet he poured, and in bitter words presignified his deadly intent to the suitors. "Thus far," he said, "this contest has been decided harmless: now for us there rests another mark, harder to hit, but which my hands shall essay notwithstanding, if Phœbus, god of archers, be pleased to give me the mastery." With that he let fly a deadly arrow at Antinous, which pierced him in the throat, as he was in the act of lifting a cup of wine to his mouth. Amazement seized the suitors, as their great champion fell dead, and they raged highly against Ulysses, and said that it should prove the dearest shaft which he ever let fly, for he had slain a man whose like breathed not in any part of the kingdom; and they flew to their arms, and would have seized the lances, but Minerva struck them with dimness of sight that they went erring up and down the hall, not knowing where to find them. Yet so infatuated were they by the displeasure of Heaven that they did not see the imminent peril which impended over them, but every man believed that this accident had happened without the intention of the doer. Fools! to think by shutting their eyes to evade destiny, or that any other cup remained for them but that which their great Antinous had tasted!

Then Ulysses revealed himself to all in that presence, and that he was the man whom they held to be dead at Troy, whose palace they had usurped, whose wife in his lifetime they had sought in impious marriage, and that for this reason destruction was come upon them. And he dealt his deadly arrows among them, and there was no avoiding him, nor escaping from his horrid person; and Telemachus by his side plied them thick with those murderous lances from which there was no retreat, till fear itself made them valiant, and danger gave them eyes to understand the peril; then they which had swords drew them, and some with shields, that could find them, and some with tables and benches snatched up in haste, rose in a mass to overwhelm and crush those two; yet they singly bestirred themselves like men, and defended themselves against that great host, and through tables, shields, and all, right through the arrows of Ulysses clove, and the irresistible lances of Telemachus; and many lay dead, and all had wounds, and Minerva in the likeness of a bird sat upon the beam which went across the hall, clapping her wings with a fearful noise; and sometimes the great bird would fly among them, cuffing at the swords and at the lances, and up and down the hall would go, beating her wings, and troubling everything, that it was frightful to behold, and it frayed the blood from the cheeks of those heaven-hated suitors; but to Ulysses and his son she appeared in her own divine similitude, with her snake-fringed shield, a goddess armed, fighting their battles. Nor did that dreadful pair desist till they had laid all their foes at their feet. At their feet they lay in shoals: like fishes, when the fishermen break up their nets, so they lay gasping and sprawling at the feet of Ulysses and his son. And Ulysses remembered the prediction of Tiresias, which said that he was to perish by his own guests, unless he slew those who knew him not.

Then certain of the queen's household went up and told Penelope what had happened, and how her lord Ulysses was come home, and had slain the suitors. But she gave no heed to their words, but thought that some frenzy possessed them, or that they mocked her; for it is the property of such extremes of sorrow as she had felt not to believe when any great joy cometh. And she rated and chid them exceedingly for troubling her. But they the more persisted in their asseverations of the truth of what they had affirmed; and some of them had seen the slaughtered bodies of the suitors dragged forth of the hall. And they said, "That poor guest whom you talked with last night was Ulysses." Then she was yet more fully persuaded that they mocked her, and she wept. But they said, "This thing is true which we have told. We sat within, in an inner room in the palace, and the doors of the hall were shut on us, but we heard the cries and the groans of the men that were killed, but saw nothing, till at length your son called to us to come in, and entering we saw Ulysses standing in the midst of the slaughtered." But she, persisting in her unbelief, said that it was some god which had deceived them to think it was the person of Ulysses.

By this time Telemachus and his father had cleansed their hands from the slaughter, and were come to where the queen was talking with those of her household; and when she saw Ulysses, she stood motionless, and had no power to speak, sudden surprise and joy and fear and many passions so strove within her. Sometimes she was clear that it was her husband that she saw, and sometimes the alteration which twenty years had made in his person (yet that was not much) perplexed her that she knew not what to think, and for joy she could not believe, and yet for joy she would not but believe; and, above all, that sudden change from a beggar to a king troubled her, and wrought uneasy scruples in her mind. But Telemachus, seeing her strangeness, blamed her, and called her an ungentle and tyrannous mother; and said that she showed a too great curiousness of modesty, to abstain from embracing his father, and to have doubts of his person, when to all present it was evident that he was the very real and true Ulysses.

Then she mistrusted no longer, but ran and fell upon

Ulysses's neck, and said, "Let not my husband be angry, that I held off so long with strange delays; it is the gods, who severing us for so long time, have caused this unseemly distance in me. If Menelaus's wife had used half my caution, she would never have taken so freely to a stranger; and she might have spared us all these plagues which have come upon us through her shameless deed."

These words with which Penelope excused herself wrought more affection in Ulysses than if upon a first sight she had given up herself implicitly to his embraces; and he wept for joy to possess a wife so discreet, so answering to his own staid mind, that had a depth of wit proportioned to his own, and one that held chaste virtue at so high a price; and he thought the possession of such a one cheaply purchased with the loss of all Circe's delights and Calypso's immortality of joys; and his long labors and his severe sufferings past seemed as nothing, now they were crowned with the enjoyment of his virtuous and true wife Penelope. And as sad men at sea whose ship has gone to pieces nigh shore, swimming for their lives, all drenched in foam and brine, crawl up to some poor patch of land, which they take possession of with as great a joy as if they had the world given them in fee, with such delight did this chaste wife cling to her lord restored, and clasp once again the living Ulysses.

So from that time the land had rest from the suitors. And the happy Ithacans with songs and solemn sacrifices of praise to the gods celebrated the return of Ulysses; for he that had been so long absent was returned to wreak the evil upon the heads of the doers; in the place where they had done the evil, there wreaked he his vengeance upon them.

In fee: for a possession.

Press of
Berwick & Smith,
Boston.

Elementary English.

CLASSICS FOR CHILDREN.

In forming the mind and taste of the young, is it not better to use authors who have already lived long enough to afford some guaranty that they may survive the next twenty years?

THIS series of standard works, edited for the use of children between the ages of nine and fifteen, was suggested by seeing the result of setting children of nine and eleven years to reading THE LADY OF THE LAKE. They soon became so much interested in it, that they began not only to read with greater ease, but voluntarily committed to memory large portions of the poem.

This result led to making numerous inquiries of thoughtful men and women, in various walks of life, in regard to their early reading. The evidence thus gained shows that children are capable of enjoying good books at an early age, and the chances of forming in them a taste for good literature are then much better than at a later period.

The child should have only the best set before him, for otherwise he is more liable to copy the imperfect, or to become confused between the true and the false, than to be guided aright.

At the same time, it is necessary for children to read a great deal, to acquire that facility of expression which will enable them to perform the merely mechanical operation of reading without conscious effort. The mind should be entirely free to concentrate itself on the subject-matter. Now, since it is not natural for them to apply themselves closely enough and long enough to accomplish this work, we should aid them by supplying an abundance of interesting material. It is, therefore, of the utmost importance, at this stage of the child's education, not only that the highest moral truths be presented, but that the matter be of such intense interest as to *catch* and *hold* the whole attention of the pupil. The highest moral law he should now know is to learn the command of words, and the most effective use of his faculties. Care should be taken that his English should be simple and forcible, and nothing harmful in ethics should be allowed. If a large portion of the time now given to spelling out words, in geography, arithmetic, grammar, and stupid scrap reading-lessons, were devoted at first to reading only, our children would not only become much better scholars in these various branches, but read more literature in the Grammar Schools than the college student now gets before graduating; besides, they would acquire a literary taste and a love for good reading, of inestimable value to them in their future life, which will never be so busy but that they will find a few moments for the gratification of it. People are ignorant, not so much because of being overworked, as from want of a love for good reading. Give the children a chance, a glimpse into the great storehouses of knowledge in books, wherein they may commune with the greatest minds at their best.

It is of the greatest importance to develop a love for history in early life, as no one can be well read without a fair knowledge of the past. In fact, one must know a people in order to understand their literature. Some of the best thoughts of a writer, depending upon allusions to historical persons or events, are entirely lost to the reader not familiar with history. Nor is this the only reason of its value. The tracing of great events unfolds the mind. We suffer and enjoy with the struggling mortals of the past, and, as it were, pass through their very experiences, and are able to reap their rewards while we avoid their mistakes. One who really loves history will *find time* to read it, but none for cheap novels. Leading epochs should be selected from the great historians, adding such information as may be necessary for a complete understanding of the extracts. The historical novel and biography are especially well calculated to create a love for history, and the whole course should be so graded that biography, natural history, novels, travels, history, and the various departments of literature should be made mutually helpful and dependent, covering the same periods and illustrating one another.

This work cannot be left to the High School, for we find, on a careful examination of the reports from several of our largest cities, where the schools have attained their greatest perfection, that only one in twenty-five of the whole number of pupils ever reaches that grade.

Besides, only a very limited portion of time is now given to this work in our higher institutions of learning, and there is a prospect of less in the near future. The bread-and-butter theory of education, appealing directly to the needs of the great majority of the people, has always exerted a strong influence against the higher training, and of late it has become alarmingly popular in our very strongholds of a liberal education.

It is hoped that this attempt to put standard literature into the hands of young children will receive encouragement, and that a free discussion of the subject may lead to such changes in the course of instruction in the Public Schools as shall give to each study the proportion of time its importance may fairly claim.

The following are ready.

Each of the volumes is printed in large type, on good paper, and firmly bound. Each is complete; or abridged, where cutting has been necessary, by a skilful hand, without impairment of style or story. Illustrations, when desirable, are freely used. The prices have been made as low as possible. As there has been a large call from the high schools for the "Lady of the Lake," "Greek Heroes," "Quentin Durward," "Stories of the Old World," "Tales of a Grandfather," and others, an edition has been bound in cloth, omitting the headline "Classics for Children," as possibly objectionable to higher classes.

Hans Andersen's Fairy Tales.

Edited for school and home use, by J. H. Stickney.

FIRST SERIES: Supplementary to the Third Reader, for children from eight to twelve years of age. 12mo. viii + 280 pp. Illustrated. Mailing prices: Cloth, 55 cents; Boards, 45 cents. For Introduction: Cloth, 50 cents; Boards, 40 cts.

SECOND SERIES: Supplementary to the Fourth Reader, for children from ten to fourteen years of age. 12mo. 000 pp. Illustrated. Mailing prices: Cloth, ; Boards, . For Introduction: Cloth, ; Boards, .

THIRD SERIES: Supplementary to the Fifth Reader, for children of twelve years and upwards, with an account of the author's life. 12mo. 000 pp. Illustrated. Mailing prices: Cloth, ; Boards, . For Introduction, Cloth, ; Boards, .

There has hitherto been no edition adapted to the wants of the varied readers to whose capacities the stories were addressed. This embarrassment is avoided by the grading of the present edition and its publication in three series. Care has been taken to winnow out everything unsuitable, and at the same time to preserve the full life of the original. Little required amendment, for both in language and spirit the stories are models. The text is based upon a sentence-by-sentence comparison of the translations current in England and America.

Æsop's Fables.

Edited by J. H. STICKNEY, with a life of Æsop, and a Supplement containing fables from La Fontaine and Krilof. 12mo. xvii + 204 pp. Illustrated. Boards: Mailing price, 40 cts.; for Introduction, 35 cts. Cloth: 60 and 50 cts.

The desire to give the Fables to children at the time in their lives when their teachings will have greatest influence, and to present them in such a style as to make them available to teachers and attractive to children, has led to the preparation of the present child's version. The book is first a Reader, then a means of language culture, and last, but by no means least, a partial manual of practical ethics.

Kingsley's Water-Babies.

Edited by J. H. STICKNEY. 12mo. 204 pages. Illustrated. Boards: Mailing price, 40 cts.; Introduction, 35 cts. Cloth: 60 and 50 cts.

Testimony to any extent might easily be adduced to the excellent style and healthy tone of this beautiful story. A slight abridgment, involving no other change than the omission of difficult passages, not intended to be understood by children, and amounting in the aggregate to less than forty in the two hundred and fifty pages, has perfectly adapted it to use in the schoolroom.

The King of the Golden River; or, The Black Brothers.

By JOHN RUSKIN. A legend of Stiria. 12mo. 54 pp. Illustrated. Boards: Mailing price, 24 cts.; for Introduction, 20 cts. Cloth: 30 and 25 cts.

A charming and wholesome fairy tale by a great author. The quaint illustrations add much to its interest.

The Swiss Family Robinson.

Edited by J. H. STICKNEY. viii + 364 pp. Illustrated. Boards: Mailing price, 50 cts.; for Introduction, 40 cts. Cloth: 60 and 50 cts.

The text has been carefully compiled from the best editions; and the Notes and Introduction will be found helpful. The story itself needs no commendation.

Robinson Crusoe.

The famous English Classic. Edited for Supplementary Reading in Schools, by W. H. LAMBERT. 12mo. 263 pages. Boards: Mailing price, 40 cts.; Introduction, 35 cts. Cloth: 60 and 50 cts.

It has been slightly abridged by the omission of unimportant matter, and ends with his leaving the island. Great care has been taken to preserve Defoe's language.

Kingsley's Greek Heroes.

Edited by JOHN TETLOW, Head Master of the Girls' High and Latin Schools, Boston. 12mo. 168 pages. Illustrated. Boards: Mailing price, 40 cts.; Introduction, 35 cts. Cloth: 55 and 50 cts.

It is surprising that this book has never before been edited for school use. It is particularly fitted to please the young, while its character and style are the very best. The lessons of heroism which it teaches in the most forcible way — by example — cannot fail of their effect.

Lamb's Tales from Shakespeare.

320 pages. Boards: Mailing price, 50 cts.; Introduction, 40 cts. Cloth: 60 and 50 cts.

Adapted to class use by the omission of "Measure for Measure," not suited for children, and by a few verbal changes. In its present form, the "Tales" will, it is hoped, be very welcome from the intrinsic interest of the stories, and the delightful way they are told.

Scott's Tales of a Grandfather.

Being the history of Scotland from the earliest period to its union with England under James VI. Abridged by EDWIN GINN. Boards: Mailing price, 50 cts.; Introduction, 40 cts. Cloth: 60 and 50 cts.

The story of a heroic age narrated in the matchless style of the great national author.

Scott's Lady of the Lake.

Edited by EDWIN GINN. 12mo. 268 pages. Boards: Mailing price, 40 cts.; Introduction, 35 cts. Cloth: 60 and 50 cts.

It contains a brief life of Scott, and his critical notes on the poem carefully abridged, with sufficient annotation to be easily read by children ten years old. It also contains a brief life of James V., as well as a full description of the Highlands and their clans during his reign. This poem, with its beautiful descriptions of scenery, its vivid pictures of life, and the charming melody of its rhythm, seems especially well suited to interest the young. The reader will be assisted to comprehend the story by the sketch map of the region printed at the end of this volume.

Stories of the Old World.

Prepared expressly for this Series by the Rev. ALFRED J. CHURCH, M.A., author of "Stories from Homer, Livy, Virgil, etc." 12mo. 354 pages. Boards: Mailing price, 50 cts.; Introduction, 40 cts. Cloth: 60 and 50 cts.

The contents comprise the stories of the Argo, Thebes, the Iliad, Odyssey, and Æneid. The style is simple, idiomatic, and easy. The book was prepared especially for Grammar School pupils, many of whom would have no other opportunity of knowing anything of these old classics. It has, however, met with no less favor in classical schools, both from the intrinsic interest of the narratives, and as affording an introduction to their Latin and Greek reading.

Scott's Talisman.

Edited by DWIGHT HOLBROOK, Principal of Morgan School, Clinton, Conn., with an Introduction by Miss Charlotte M. Yonge. 12mo. xii + 454 pp. Boards: Mailing price, 60 cts.; Introduction, 50 cts. Cloth: 70 and 60 cts.

The Talisman serves a double purpose, both as introducing Scott to youth and affording a graphic account of an important period of history. It is here given without abridgment.

In this work are found in vivid contrast two distinct civilizations, — that of the East and West. The notes, which are of two kinds, — historical and explanatory, — supply information tending to deepen the interest in the story and its prominent actors.

Scott's Quentin Durward.

Edited for this Series, with an Historical Introduction, by CHARLOTTE M. YONGE, of England. 12mo. 312 pages. Boards: Mailing price, 50 cts.; Introduction, 40 cts. Cloth: 60 and 50 cts.

In this edition the violence of the old times is mitigated, while the interest of the story, and its lessons of fidelity, courage, and sturdy manhood, are not weakened.

Irving's Sketch Book.

With full notes, questions, etc., for home and school use. By HOMER B. SPRAGUE, Ph.D., and M. E. SCATES, of the Girls' High School, Boston. 12mo. 126 pages. Boards: Mailing price, 30 cents; for Introduction, 25 cents. Cloth: Mailing price, 40 cents; for Introduction, 35 cents.

The volume comprises *The Voyage, Westminster Abbey, The Widow and her Son, Rip Van Winkle, The Legend of Sleepy Hollow,* and *Christmas.* For further description, see p. 51.

Shakespeare's Merchant of Venice.

HUDSON and LAMB. 12mo. 115 pages. Boards: Mailing price, 30 cts.; Introduction, 25 cts. Cloth: 45 and 40 cts.

It contains Hudson's Life of Shakespeare, and about two-thirds of the Text and Notes of his School Edition, and Lamb's Story of the play. None of the omissions impair the value of the work for children.

Scott's Guy Mannering.

Edited with notes, and a historical introduction by Miss CHARLOTTE M. YONGE. 12mo. 000 pp. Boards: Mailing price,   ; for Introduction,   . Cloth: Mailing price,   ; for Introduction,

No remarks need be made upon the interest of this book, or its suitableness for use as a reader. It is given without abridgement.

Scott's Ivanhoe.

Edited with notes, and a historical introduction by Miss CHARLOTTE M. YONGE. 12mo. 000 pp. Boards: Mailing price,   ; for Introduction,   . Cloth: Mailing price,   ; for Introduction,

Like the Talisman and Guy Mannering, Ivanhoe is given complete.

[*Ready*]   , 1886.

ENGLISH GRAMMAR.

Elementary Lessons in English. Part First:

"*HOW TO SPEAK AND WRITE CORRECTLY.*" By Mrs. N. L. KNOX-HEATH. (*Teacher's edition described below.*) 12mo. Cloth. 192 pages. Mailing price, 50 cents; Introduction, 45 cents; Allowance, 15 cents.

This Part contains *no technical grammar*. It is designed to give children such a knowledge of the English Language as will enable them to *speak*, *write*, and *use* it with accuracy and force. It is made up of exercises to increase and improve the vocabulary, lessons in enunciation, pronunciation, spelling, sentence-making, punctuation, the use of capitals, abbreviations, drill in writing number-forms, gender-forms, and the possessive-form, letter-writing, and such other matters pertaining to the art of the language as may be taught simply, clearly, and profitably. Many and varied oral and written exercises supplement every lesson.

The Teacher's Edition of Elementary Lessons

in English. To accompany PART I.: "*HOW TO SPEAK AND WRITE CORRECTLY.*" Prepared by Mrs. N. L. KNOX. 12mo. Cloth. 323 pages. Mailing price, 70 cts.; Introduction price, 60 cts.

The "Teacher's Edition" contains the entire text of the children's book, and, in addition, plans for developing the lessons of the text, observation lessons, dictation and test exercises, questions for oral and written reviews, materials for composition exercises, plans for conducting picture lessons, a story lesson, etc., etc., etc.

In a preliminary chapter (*The Teacher's Guide*) will be found a discussion of the Pestalozzian principles of education and instruction, of the art of questioning and the laws of questioning, of methods of correcting oral and written mistakes, and of oral lessons — how to prepare them, and how to give them. This includes also material and plans for Oral Lessons in Language for the first, second, third, and fourth years in school. There is no book published in this country which is so clear, direct, and complete a manual for the use of teachers.

These books are endorsed by leading educators in every part of the country. They have stood the test of the school-room. Teachers and pupils unite in their praise. The following testimonials to their merits and usefulness, selected from our *Special Circular*, were chosen as a fair geographical representation of public opinion rather than as the strongest endorsements which the Circular contains : —

Dr. G. Stanley Hall, *Prof. of Psychology and Pedagogy, Johns Hopkins Univ.:* At present, when some of the fundamental principles of treating the vernacular have been opened for discussion and involved in doubt, it is no easy matter to write a text-book which shall harmonize and utilize most if not all of the practical advantages claimed for conflicting theories. This is accomplished in these admirable books to a surprising degree. They will surely find wide acceptation, as they deserve to.

J. W. Babcock, *Supt. of Schools, Dunkirk, N.Y.:* No book of its kind has ever given us such wonderful results. Pupils study it with *pleasure* as well as with profit. In fact it is no uncommon circumstance for an entire class to remain after school and urge the teacher to develop *extra* work for the next day.

John B. Peaslee, *Supt. of Schools, Cincinnati, O.:* It meets my views on that subject better than any other work I have seen.

S. G. Taylor, *late Prin. Adelphi Acad., Brooklyn, N.Y.:* We have used the "Elementary Lessons in English" for the past year, with great satisfaction, and consider it the best work on this subject that we have ever seen.

H. Courthope Bowen, *Prin. Finnsbury Training College, London, Eng.:* The plan of the book is excellent, and the Teacher's Edition is admirable.

J. A. MacCabe, *Prin. of Normal School, Ottawa, Can.:* The simplicity as well as originality with which the subject is treated really take the book far out of the ordinary class of grammars and language lessons. The intrinsic worth of the book will make it in universal demand, and the whole series will be eagerly sought after when thoroughly known.

S. T. Dutton, *Supt. of Schools, New Haven, Conn.:* The introduction of Elementary Lessons in English into the New Haven Schools marked an era in our manner of teaching language. Many teachers had previously used the book for reference, and found its methods to be sound, and its suggestions helpful. Now the "Teacher's Edition" is in the hands of all teachers, and the pupil's edition is used in all classes below the sixth grade. I think we have reason to be grateful both to the author and publisher of this work. (*Jan.* 18, 1883.)

Prof. W. G. Williams, *Wesleyan Univ., Delaware, O., and Member State Board of Examiners:* I have no hesitancy in recommending this as the best text-book on this subject within my knowledge. We have introduced the work into the public schools of this city.

Henry E. Shepherd, *Supt. of Schools, Baltimore, Md.:* The general design of the work commends itself very strongly to my favor. I am especially pleased with the "Teacher's Guide."

S. W. Mason, *Board of Supervisors, Boston, Mass.:* The entire book is a most valuable contribution to show teachers *what* to do and how to do it, and it will prove to be an excellent text-book upon the subjects so intelligently and practically presented.

Albert L. Bacheller, *Prin. of Grammar School, Lowell, Mass.:* There has never been a text-book employed in my school in any branch of study which has given greater satisfaction.

F. Louis Soldan, *Prin. Normal School, St. Louis, Mo.:* The highest scholarship and the best talent and professional ability in teaching united to give us these books.
(*Feb.* 21, 1882.)

W. N. Barringer, *Supt. of Schools, Newark, N.J.:* We use it entirely in our primary grades, and in the fourth grade grammar department. It gives the best of satisfaction.

A. W. Mell, *Prin. Nor. Sch., Bowling Green, Ky.:* In the light of present attainments in language teaching, the plan seems a *ne plus ultra*. The "Teacher's Edition" affords a most valuable help in methods of teaching; not only in language, but any other branch as well.

J. W. Thompson, *County Examiner, Conway, Ark.:* No teacher should be without it. As a text-book in the hands of pupils, I can only say that I believe it to be the shortest and easiest road to a knowledge of the English language.

David Beattie, *Supt. of Schools, Troy, N.Y.:* Your book is really a good one, perhaps the only one worthy its name. In the hands of an honest and industrious teacher, the "Teacher's Edition" will prove a small normal school in itself.

D. H. Darling, *Supt. of Schools, Joliet, Ill.:* We all agree that it is the most excellent, practical, and useful book on language for primary teachers that we have ever seen.

Geo. Howland, *Supt. of Schools, Chicago:* I know of no work on the subject more suggestive and helpful to the young teacher.

J. H. Haldeman, *Prin. School of Observation, State Normal School, Westfield, Mass.:* The interest increases as the pupil advances, and the results are most satisfactory. (*Mar.* 10, 1882.)

J. Ormond Wilson, *Supt. of Public Schools, Washington, D.C.:* It has been used in the public schools of the District since Sept. 1, 1880, and has given the best satisfaction.

A. L. Purinton, *Supt. of Schools, Parkersburg, W. Va.:* We are using it in these schools, and every day's experience adds its testimony to its excellence and fitness in the real work of the school-room. It is well-nigh faultless.

C. F. Gunther, *St. Louis, Mo.:* I find the "Elementary Lessons" *especially* good with German children.

www.ingramcontent.com/pod-product-compliance
Lightning Source LLC
Chambersburg PA
CBHW021939160426
43195CB00011B/1148